The BORROWER'S ANSWER BOOK

ALSO BY GAIL VAZ-OXLADE

THE RRSP ANSWER BOOK

The BORROWER'S ANSWER BOOK

GAIL VAZ-OXLADE

First published in 1993 by
Stoddart Publishing Co. Limited
34 Lesmill Road
Toronto, Canada
M3B 2T6
(416) 445-3333

Canadian Cataloguing in Publication Data

Vaz-Oxlade, Gail E., 1959–
The borrower's answer book

Includes index.
ISBN 0-7737-5587-X

1. Loans, Personal — Canada.   2. Consumer credit —
Canada.   3. Finance, Personal — Canada.   I. Title.

HG3756.C3V39 1993   332.7   C93-094416-X

Cover design: Brant Cowie/ArtPlus
Printed and bound in Canada

Stoddart Publishing gratefully acknowledges the support of
the Canada Council, The Ontario Ministry of Culture,
Tourism, and Recreation, Ontario Arts Council, and Ontario
Publishing Centre in the development of writing and
publishing in Canada.

Contents

3 Mortgages

Introduction

To borrow or not to borrow?

This is one of the most loudly debated questions. Everyone knows someone who has fallen prey to "easy credit" and overextended themselves. I had a girlfriend who used to sit at the kitchen table trying to decide which credit cards to make minimum payments on, and which would have to wait until next month. She simply couldn't keep up with her debt.

There are lots of books written about the evils of borrowing (never borrow), how to get out of debt (stop borrowing) and how to stay out of debt (never ever borrow again). The fact is, credit is a way of life and if we try to live without it, it becomes very hard to accomplish our goals. After all, does anyone you know have the cash to buy their first home outright? If you want to buy a house, you'll probably have to finance it. The same is true if you want to buy a car, or a boat, or a new kitchen. The fact is, credit isn't bad. How we use credit is the problem.

If you grew up during the thirties, forties or fifties, you probably grew up in a house where borrowing had a bad name. Our parents recognized that they had to save. They paid cash for almost everything they bought. They were willing to wait until they were well-established before they bought a house. If you grew up in the sixties, seventies or eighties, you probably grew up in a house where borrowing was considered the only way to get ahead. People leveraged investments. They took on huge debt loads. They wanted it all — TODAY!

The road that runs somewhere in the middle of these two extremes is the best path to take. The difficulty is that most people don't understand how to use credit to *their* advantage. They react to their circumstances, and they keep reacting as they get further and further into debt. When the debt becomes unmanageable, they throw their arms up in despair and say that credit is evil. Well, it's not. Well-planned borrowing can be a useful way to realize dreams and achieve financial goals. Well-planned borrowing can get you where you want to be. But it takes a good understanding of how credit works, when to use credit, and which type of credit will make borrowing work for you.

Often, when I begin to talk about credit, people have a number of reactions. Some run and hide. Others curse a blue streak, flailing their arms. Some smile smugly — it seems they know the secrets of credit.

I believe if we understand credit, we can learn how to use it to our best advantage. So here it is — *The Borrower's Answer Book:* everything you wanted to know about borrowing, but were afraid to ask. We'll look at:

- the different forms of credit available
- the right time to borrow, and which type of credit to use
- how you can prepare for your credit interview
- how to manage credit to your best advantage.

I remember walking into a trust company one day to do some routine transactions when the branch manager cornered me. Evidently the push was on to sell Personal Lines of Credit (PLCs). Wouldn't I like a personal line of credit? Did I know how convenient and discreet a PLC was? Wouldn't I want a source of credit that offered the lowest rate of interest?

I informed Mr. Branch Manager that "I don't buy credit." (That's not exactly the truth, but it's what I told him.) He looked at me aghast.

"Don't buy credit!"

"That's right," I said.

"What about if you see that perfect piece of furniture and you don't have the cash?" he asked.

"I don't buy it," I replied.

"Pardon me?"

"I don't buy it," I said, "not until I've saved the money."
Mr. Branch Manager shook his head and walked away. Clearly I was a lost case.

You see, I believe that when you enter a loan arrangement with a financial institution, you're *buying* credit. After all, you're paying interest (that's the markup) and in return you get to use the money for your enjoyment (that's what you're buying). Most financial institutions believe they "grant" credit — and they do. But from a consumer perspective, if you think about it as "buying" credit, then you're much more likely to apply all the same criteria to the purchase of credit as you would to any purchase:

- Do you really need it?
- Are you willing to pay the price asked?
- What else do you have to give up to buy this?
- Is it the best deal going?
- Is the price negotiable?
- Does this store-keeper (lender) deserve my business?

The first step is understanding the various types of credit available and how you can use them to your advantage. Since a credit card is the most popular choice of credit, we'll start there.

1 Credit Cards

If I could show you a way to borrow $5,000 a month and pay no interest, would you be curious? What if I told you that credit cards offer you the cheapest form of credit available? It's true, and here's why.

Credit cards only charge interest when your balance has not been paid off in full. If you pay off your balance each month, you pay no interest. You've used the financial institution's money for anywhere from 30 days to 60 days — and it cost you absolutely nothing.

Who Should Have a Credit Card?

Everyone. The fact is, the only people who can borrow money without going through hoops or signing away their firstborns are people who *have* borrowed money. You can't develop a "credit rating" until you have paid back a loan. A credit rating is your *reputation* in terms of your previous ability to pay back money you've borrowed in a responsible and timely way. If you've been consistently late in making your payments, you'll have a bad credit reputation, or "rep." If you've ever missed a payment completely, you'll have an even worse rep. If you've always made your payments on time, you will have a great credit rating and just about anyone will be willing to lend to you under the right circumstances.

A credit card is one of the easiest ways to establish a credit rating. Whether it is a gas card, a store card or a bank card, you can apply for a card with a low limit, make small purchases, pay off the card each month and become a credit star. You'll establish yourself in the world of credit, and you'll develop a great reputation.

What Other Ways Can You Establish a Credit Rating?

You can take out a loan. If you are a first-time borrower, you may need a guarantor to get the loan. The guarantor is a person who has established a credit reputation and who guarantees to repay the loan if you don't. You can borrow money using a guarantor and pay back that money on time to establish a credit rating. If you can't get a guarantor, and you have collateral, you can use that to secure the loan. Collateral is an asset, such as a term deposit, Canada Savings Bond or automobile, which you offer as security for the loan. If you don't repay the loan, the financial institution will seize the asset pledged as collateral and sell it or cash it in order to repay the loan.

What Do You Mean, "No"!

Sometimes the process of getting a credit card seems mysterious. Occasionally, people who have been granted a $20,000 loan (e.g., to buy a car) are then rejected for a credit card with a $5,000 limit. This can be confusing.

The misunderstanding arises because most people see a credit card (which is revolving credit) as being the same as a personal loan (which is instalment credit). These two types of credit have very different characteristics and are treated differently by financial institutions when they are determining whether or not to approve your application.

While an instalment loan is for a fixed dollar amount and term with a regular payment schedule, a revolving credit account, such as a credit card, is open-ended and may be used whenever you want for a variety of purchases or a cash advance. As well, credit cards are generally completely unsecured. (Some are secured and we'll look at these later.)

While most people don't see the difference, statistics show that people treat them quite differently when it comes to repayment. People's priorities in terms of repayment are usually:

1. mortgages
2. instalment loans
3. revolving lines of credit, such as credit cards

This means that should your financial circumstances change, you will be more likely to make your mortgage and instalment loan payments than your credit card payments. So credit cards run the highest risk of default. As a result, financial institutions consider all the information on your credit application very carefully before giving you a card.

Credit cards offer people what appears to be easy credit. With minimum payment requirements, credit cards can actually be detrimental to your credit rating if misused.

Some people don't even think of using a credit card as borrowing. After all, there's no long approval process each time you want to charge something. You just charge it and *cachunk, cachunk*. That's why financial institutions are so careful. That's also why credit limit increases are only considered once you have demonstrated an ability to manage your current limit. And that's one reason the interest rate charged on a credit card is so much higher than on other forms of credit. The second reason is fraud.

Credit card issuers experience enormous problems with fraud. They have to cover their losses in some way, and a higher rate of interest is one way to do it. Perhaps if the use of a Personal Identification Number (PIN) or a photo ID on the card becomes a standard, issuers will see fraud costs drop and we will benefit with reduced interest rates. But that's the future.

Most financial institutions use a sophisticated tool to help make the best credit-granting decision. Referred to as "credit scoring," the system assesses a number of items on your application form and gives you points for each item based on the institution's past experience with similar customers. The points are totalled to obtain a credit score. Using credit scoring, the credit decision is based on a combination of factors, rather than just one or two factors. Customers who meet the minimum score requirement are granted a credit card and assigned a starting credit limit.

When Should I Get My First Credit Card?

As soon as possible. Having said that it may be difficult to get a credit card, once you've had one and established a good credit rating, you will always be able to get another or have your limit raised.

Can I Get a Credit Card If I'm a Student?

Some credit card companies offer cards to students. The reason they do this is to initiate relationships with people they hope, over the long term, will be loyal to their company. The initial credit limit may be low, but that doesn't matter. If you can get it, take it. Be careful using it. Your objective is to build a credit reputation, not charge everything in sight.

I've Never Had a Credit Card in My Own Name. What Do I Do?

Some people have difficulty establishing that they even exist when it comes to getting credit. If you are a married woman and all the cards are in your husband's name, even if you make the payments on the card, you're contributing to his credit rating, not your own. The card company doesn't care who signed the cheques. They base their reporting to the credit bureau on whose name the card is held in.

Women who are recently divorced or widowed often face the shock that they don't exist simply because all the credit reporting was done in their husbands' names. If you are a married woman, make sure you have at least one credit card in your own name. You'll have to apply for it and qualify for it on your own. Initially, you may have to use a secured credit card (see page 16). However you get your card, make sure you use it wisely so that the reputation you develop is a good one.

The other way to become known is to open up a chequing account with your local financial institution and get to know the branch manager. You'd be surprised at how far a personal relationship with a banker can take you. After all, the more familiar she is with you, the more likely you are to get the service you want, when you want it — including getting credit.

If you're new to the workforce or a recent immigrant, the same advice applies. Establish a relationship with a financial institution, borrow some money (using a guarantor, if necessary) and start building your rep.

What's the Difference between a Credit Card and a Charge Card?

There's a big difference. A credit card such as VISA or MasterCard offers you a line of credit for which they charge you interest if you don't pay off the balance each month. A charge card, such as American Express, also allows you to charge purchases up to a specified limit. However, charge card companies expect to be paid immediately upon billing, since it is not their intention to offer you credit.

Credit Card Interest

You can avoid paying interest on your credit card for transactions (i.e., for everything other than cash advances) by making a full payment on or before the due date on your statement. However, interest is always charged on cash advances from the date you take the money. If your credit card allows you to write cheques against it, interest is charged on those types of cash advances from the date the cheque is processed to your account. And, of course, no one pays you interest if you have a credit balance on your credit or charge card account — so don't.

The Hidden Interest Charge

Interest is typically calculated on a daily basis if your account has an outstanding balance. Interest calculations begin on transactions the day the transaction is posted to your account, usually within a few days of having made the purchase. However, if you pay the total balance indicated on your statement on or before the due date, no interest will be charged.

> Marnie Worldman charged $1,000 on her credit card last month. She paid her balance in full by her payment due date, so she was not charged any interest. Her sister Deborah also charged $1,000 last month. However, Deborah made a partial payment of $400 on the due date so:
>
> - she was still charged interest on the full $1,000 up to the day the $400 was credited, since she had not completely paid off her balance, and
>
> - the remaining balance of $600 became the "retail revolving balance," which would continue to accrue interest until it was repaid.

Even through Deborah paid off $400 by the due date, she was still charged interest on the total $1,000 up until the date the $400 payment was made. That's because when you make only a partial payment, you are charged interest on the *total* balance. The only way to avoid paying any interest is to pay off your balance in full every month.

The Cost of Borrowing on a Credit Card

It's amazing how many people run balances on their credit cards when the interest rates they're charged are so high. About one in two card holders run a balance — paying interest rates from 14 to 24 percent.

Financial statistics show that most people will go out of their way to earn one-half to three-quarters percent more on a GIC. Yet we'll pay seven to 14 percent more interest than necessary, just because it's a credit card. If you have an outstanding balance of $1,000 on which you're paying 17 percent, that's costing you more than $14 a month, or almost $169 a year. And that's after tax dollars! You'd have to have a $1,000 GIC paying better than 24 percent to break even. Now, where can you find a GIC paying 24 percent in today's market?

Instead of carrying a balance on your credit card, you'd be better off taking a loan at 10 percent and paying off your credit card. If you'd go out of your way to earn one-half percent more in interest, how far out of your way would you go to save seven percent in interest costs? Fact is, you don't have to go far — just to your nearest financial institution. What are you waiting for?

How Are My Payments Applied?

When payments are received, your account is credited with the payments in the following priority:

- Previously billed
    - interest
    - cash advances
    - purchases, fees and charges that are interest-bearing
    - purchases, fees and charges that are not yet interest-bearing
- To be billed (or "unbilled")
    - cash advances
    - purchases, fees and charges

If you look at each of these as buckets, it's easier to understand how your payments are applied.

Once the first bucket, "previously billed interest," is reduced to zero (emptied), payments are applied to the second bucket, "previously billed cash advances," and so on until all your payment dollars have been applied.

On the next statement date, the credit card system checks to see if all the buckets (except "to be billed purchases") are zero and, if so, the interest accrued on the retail balance is waived.

Interest calculated on a cash advance is NEVER waived, regardless of whether a full or partial payment is made. When partial payments are made, interest accrues on the reduced principal and is charged on the next statement.

All the Extras

Credit cards offer you lots of extras that make them attractive. They can offer savings on travel insurance, car rentals and travel expenses. For example, if you have a card that offers a "car rental collision and loss damage insurance waiver," you can decline to purchase the insurance offered by a car rental agency. This can save you up to $12 a day and can cover the annual cost of a card in just a few days.

Some credit cards offer medical coverage while you're travelling. This may not only save you money, but provide you with the convenience and peace of mind of knowing that coverage is automatic. However, there are usually limitations on the length of the trips covered. Check the insurance certificate carefully before you decide to buy.

Some credit cards offer insurance on the goods you buy so if they are lost, stolen or damaged, they will be fixed or replaced free. Some even offer you a rebate when your balance is paid so you can save on your overall purchases.

❋ ❋

Instead of buying extended warranties when you buy electronics or appliances, use a credit card that offers extended protection. You can have the normal manufacturer's warranty on most items doubled (sometimes to a maximum of one additional year) simply by using the right credit card. You save money by not buying an extended warranty — and if you pay your card off on time, it costs you absolutely nothing.

❋ ❋

Some cards offer bonus points redeemable for merchandise; others have an affiliation with an airline that earns you travel points. Take advantage of these special characteristics to make your life easier and to save money. If you travel a lot, for example, then a credit card that offers special travel features may be the right one for you. These features may include:

- trip interruption, delay and/or cancellation insurance
- baggage loss/delay insurance
- hotel burglary insurance
- guaranteed reservations

Most credit cards offer a card registry service that sometimes includes the registration of important documents (e.g., passports, birth certificates, etc.) so you can retrieve those numbers any time with one phone call. If you've ever lost your wallet while travelling, you know what a pain it can be to contact all the proper authorities to report your missing cards. With the card registry service, it's done for you.

Some cards even offer insurance on the balance owing so that your balance will be paid off in the event of involuntary job loss or death.

Each insurance coverage package has exclusions and restrictions, and the details can be found in the individual insurance certificates. Take the time to clearly understand the terms and conditions for the insurance coverage offered before you decide on a credit card.

Don't Forget the Fees

Many credit cards charge a transaction fee or an annual fee. Prices range dramatically. Some cards have no fees, but these usually don't offer any of the special features just described.

When you're trying to decide which card is best for you, weigh the fee charged against how often you will be using the card. It may be less expensive to have one credit card for which you pay an annual fee for all your purchases than several credit cards for which you pay transaction fees. Perhaps the best solution is one card with all the bells and whistles that suit your needs, for which you will likely pay a fee, and one with no fee at all, which you can use as a backup, if necessary. Remember, not all cards are accepted at all retail locations, so having two different types of cards can be a distinct advantage.

Using Credit Cards Wisely

Credit cards are a great way to begin establishing a credit rating. If you find you are a nonentity in the world of credit, get yourself a credit card, start charging, and pay off your balance every month. After about six months, see if you can get your limit raised. Remember, though, not paying off your balance on time will cost you significantly in interest. Failing to make even the minimum monthly payment will cost you on your credit rating.

Credit cards are extremely convenient. They're safer than carrying scads of cash, and they are easier to use than personal cheques. If you pay them off on time, they can be even cheaper than using cheques. There's no question that cards have a place in your credit closet, but you have to be disciplined in managing them, or they can turn ugly.

Choose your credit cards carefully. Some charge higher interest than others. Store cards are notorious for charging the highest interest. Besides which, what do you need a store card for if you have a financial institution's card? It's just a temptation to spend more than you have. And it's hard to keep track when you have zillions of cards at your disposal. Get rid of them. Keep only those you can manage effectively.

Getting Rid of Your High-Cost Debt

Do you have a credit card balance on which you're paying between 17 and 30 percent interest? Do you know what that's actually costing you? If you have a $2,500 balance on your credit card, and you're paying 17 percent interest, it's costing you $425 a year, or $35.41 a month. And that's after tax dollars. In real before-tax dollars, at a marginal tax rate of 41 percent, you're paying about $600 a year, or $50 a month. Don't you have at least a dozen things you'd rather do with that $50 a month?

Often people who carry debt also have savings or investments on which they earn much less interest than they're paying on their debt. Do you have money in a savings account earning four percent or less? Have you bought Canada Savings Bonds paying six percent? You'd be much better off using that money to pay off your high-cost debt. For example, if you have $2,500 in a CSB paying six percent, you're earning $150 a

year in interest, before tax. Compared with the $600 a year (before tax) you're spending to carry your credit card balance, you're losing $450 a year. If you cashed in that CSB and paid off your credit card, you'd actually end up $450 ahead.

Paying off your high-cost debt is one of the best investments you can make. Don't be so concerned about having a security net that you fail to use your resources to your best advantage. Start thinking about your money in terms of how much you actually have, as opposed to how much you owe and how much you've saved. Look at the big picture and then make the decisions necessary to paint that big picture black. Get out of the red! Pay off your debts.

❁ ❁

Did you know that when you borrow money to make an investment, the interest on that money is tax deductible? Let's say, for example, you sold some stock to pay off a $2,500 debt at 17 percent. You'd be saving $450 a year in interest costs. If you borrowed $2,500 to buy back that stock and paid 10 percent interest on the loan, that loan would cost you about $250 a year. So, you could pay off your high-cost debt, have your stock and still save $200 a year in interest costs.

❁ ❁

Using Credit Cards to *Your* Advantage

The key to using credit cards to your advantage is *never charge more than you can afford to pay*. One trick is to use your chequebook register to keep track of your charges. Each time you charge an item on your credit card, deduct it from your balance in your chequebook register. That way, you're always working with the actual amount of money you have. Then, when the bill comes in, write the number of the cheque used to pay the bill (or the date the bill was paid) against each of the transactions for which you are paying.

Keep in mind that not all transactions are processed to your account every month. Using the chequebook register is a great way to keep track of how much you are spending, how much you actually have, and as a double-check to ensure you are not being charged for transactions you didn't make.

Protecting Yourself against Fraud

Credit card security is one issue both credit card companies and their customers are concerned about. Since their introduction, credit cards have changed the way we pay for goods and services. It is estimated that three out of every four adult Canadians use at least one credit card. In fact, on average, adult Canadians have four credit or charge cards. With so many cards in existence, misuse is a significant risk, and statistics show that credit card crime is growing.

Many credit card companies offer you protection in the event your card is lost or stolen and used fraudulently. The option for "limited liability" for unauthorized use of the card must usually be requested (unless you have a really heads-up salesperson), and the protection is only valid when a lost or stolen card is reported immediately. If you follow the rules, your liability is usually limited to a maximum of only $50. Take advantage of this limited liability protection, and remember to report lost or stolen cards immediately.

Don't leave your credit cards in high-risk theft areas such as your workplace, in the glove compartment of your car, sitting out in the open while on public transportation, or in health clubs and hospitals. If your card is lost or stolen, report it immediately. Since most lost or stolen cards are fraudulently used immediately after they are stolen, prompt reporting can make a big difference. The telephone number for reporting lost or stolen cards is usually provided on the back of your credit card statement.

Don't keep your PIN (personal identification number) with your credit cards. The "limited liability" protection mentioned earlier is not extended to cash advances — even those that are fraudulent. Protect yourself. No one should have access to your PIN but you.

Be very careful about giving out your credit card number over the telephone. Phony companies calling to solicit travel business or sell products may encourage you to give them your credit card number. Later, you may find that your account has been charged for products or services you neither requested nor received. While there are many legitimate telemarketing companies and survey companies, you should only give the number out when the organization is known to you and the product or service is one you have requested.

Whenever you use your card, keep your copy of the receipt so that you have an actual record of the transaction. Tear up your carbons so someone rustling through the garbage won't find your name, number and signature. Put some sort of identifying mark on your card. Sometimes cards get mixed up by busy sales clerks. If your card has a distinctive mark (borrow a sticker from one of your kids), you'll be able to instantly recognize it.

Take a photocopy of all your credit cards so you have a record of all the details of your cards if they are lost or stolen. Remember to keep those records in a safe place.

And finally, when your card expires and you get a replacement card in the mail, cut up your old card. Don't just cut it in half; cut it along the numbers, and chop it into small pieces. The likelihood of anyone finding all the pieces is much smaller that way.

What If You Have Trouble Making Your Payments?

It happens to the best of us. There are lots of books written about getting out of debt and there's a good reason. It's far easier to get into debt than to get out of debt. If you run into trouble making your credit card (or any type of credit) payments, you can get out. It just takes time.

Begin by calling the credit card company and explaining the problem. If you've lost your job, or become ill and are not working, tell the credit card company. If you are simply in over your head, tell the credit card company. The important thing is to *tell the credit card company.* They would much rather talk to you than send you nasty letters and wonder if they will ever be paid. You will probably be able to work out a repayment plan. You may even be able to negotiate with them to reduce the total amount you owe if you make a full payment.

> Jani Lewis was desperate. She was laid off six months earlier and her credit cards were up to their limits. Her ex-husband hadn't given her any child support for almost a year. She didn't even know where he was. She owed $3,400 to VISA and $2,200 to MasterCard. She didn't have enough to make even the minimum monthly payment. She also owed almost $800 on two store cards, and she hadn't made her car payments in almost three months. She was just starting a new job, but didn't see any way of ever being able to catch up. I suggested she call her creditors and try to work something out. She did, and they were happy to co-operate.
>
> One company set up a payment schedule with her. She could pay $50 a month until she was caught up provided she didn't charge any more on the card. Another agreed to accept a single payment of half of what she owed if paid immediately. She borrowed $1,100 from her mom, which took care of that problem. She called her bank and explained her position. Since she only had six months left on her loan, they agreed to refinance her loan adding the $800 she owed the stores so she could have one single payment she could work into her cash flow. Her dad co-signed the loan and she promised to get on a budget. She was on her way to recovery.

Now, not everyone has a mom or dad willing to bail her out. Jani was lucky. But the steps she took apply to just about everyone:

1. Contact your creditors and tell them what's happening.
2. Try to work out a payment plan that fits with your cash flow.
3. See if the creditor will take less if you agree to make a single repayment.
4. See if your bank will agree to give you a consolidation loan. By doing this you can save a good deal of interest.
5. Put yourself on a budget.

Re-establishing Your Credit Rating

Whenever you fall off the track, your credit rating gets bruised. If you want to be considered a good risk, you have to work at re-establishing your credit rating. One way is to get a secured credit card and make your payments faithfully. A secured credit card is one that is fully secured, meaning there's no risk to the credit card company. What you do is provide the credit card company with enough cash to cover your balance. Financial institutions typically want twice the amount of credit you're asking for. So if you want a credit card with a $500 balance, you must put up $1,000 in cash. After you've made regular payments for about a year or so, the financial institution will drop the security requirement and return your deposit.

2 Loans

Apart from credit cards, there are five basic categories of credit:

- instalment loans
- demand loans
- personal lines of credit (PLCs) or home equity lines of credit (HELCs)
- overdraft protection
- mortgages

Since mortgages are really a different kettle of fish, we'll concentrate on the first four types and deal with mortgages in chapter 3.

What Is an Instalment Loan?

An instalment loan is the typical loan you take out to finance such major purchases as a car, appliances or a new roof. It is a loan of a fixed amount that requires regular payments. These payments can be made weekly, bi-weekly, semi-monthly and/or monthly. There are two types of instalment loans: fixed-rate and variable-rate.

Fixed-Rate Instalment Loans

With a fixed-rate instalment loan, the conditions and interest rate are set for the term of the loan and payments are usually blended. That means the payments are set up as a blend of principal and interest designed to repay the loan in total by the end of the term. For example, if you borrow $5,000 at 10 percent, you'll pay a total of $500 in interest in the first year, assuming the interest isn't calculated on a declining balance. That means that over one year you'll make total payments of $5,500, or $458.33 a month.

Many financial institutions calculate the interest on your loan on the declining balance. To understand how this works, you have to look at the principal (i.e., the amount you borrowed) and the interest (the cost of the loan) as two separate payments. For example, if you borrow $5,000 at 10 percent on January 1 and your payments are $400 a month, this is how your monthly payments would be applied:

	Outstanding Balance	Monthly Interest	Monthly Payment	Applied to Principal	Principal Balance
February 1	$5,000.00	$41.66	$400.00	$358.34	$4,641.66
March 1	4,641.66	38.68	400.00	361.32	4,280.34
April 1	4,280.34	35.66	400.00	364.34	3,916.00
May 1	3,916.00	32.63	400.00	367.37	3,548.63
June 1	3,548.63	29.57	400.00	370.43	3,178.20
July 1	3,178.20	26.48	400.00	373.52	2,804.68
August	2,804.68	23.37	400.00	376.63	2,428.65
September 1	2,428.65	20.23	400.00	379.77	2,048.88
October 1	2,048.88	17.07	400.00	382.93	1,665.95
November 1	1,665.95	13.88	400.00	386.12	1,279.83
December 1	1,279.83	10.66	400.00	389.34	890.49
January 1	890.49	7.42	400.00	392.58	497.91
February 1	497.91	4.14	400.00	395.86	102.05
March 1	102.05	0.85	101.20	101.20	0.00

As you can see, since your principal goes down each month, the amount of interest you pay also goes down so that more of your payment goes to paying off the principal. Financial institutions calculate the interest on the declining balance from the outset, so the lender will provide you with a monthly payment amount that will pay off the loan in the term you request.

With a blended payment, you know exactly how much your payments will be each month, and how long it will take to pay off the loan so you can work the payments into your budget.

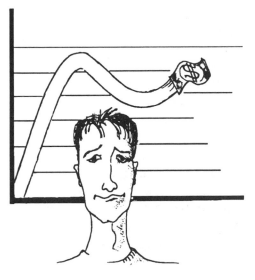

Variable-Rate Instalment Loans

Variable- or floating-rate instalment loans provide you with maximum flexibility during periods when interest rates are declining. The rate of interest charged fluctuates with changes in market conditions. For example, if you take a loan in January at 10 percent and in mid-month the interest rates fall, then the interest rate charged on your loan in February would be adjusted down to reflect the lower rate. Typically, though, the amount of your payments doesn't change. Instead, more of your payment is applied to the principal since less is needed to cover the interest.

With floating-rate loans, the interest rate is not fixed. Rather it "floats" with the prime lending rate. Prime is the lowest rate a financial institution charges its best customers — usually their corporate customers since they tend to borrow considerably higher amounts than most individuals. We common folk usually pay several points above prime. The more valued you are as a customer, the lower the interest rate you'll be charged.

❋ ❋

By establishing a long-term relationship with one or two financial institutions, you can become a valued customer. The more business you do with a single financial institution, the more valued you will be. For example, if one company has your mortgage, your chequing and savings accounts, most of your investment dollars in term deposits and mutual funds, and your retirement savings (i.e., RRSPs), that

company will work a lot harder to keep you as a customer. They have a lot to lose if you move to another financial institution.

Whenever you're trying to negotiate a loan, offer to consolidate your business with the financial institution in exchange for a lower rate of interest. Go to your interview prepared to show what a great customer you could be. If you already deal with a single financial institution, shop around to see what another financial institution would give to get your business. Remember, you are the customer, and it is ultimately up to you who gets your business. In today's highly competitive marketplace, you have every right to expect financial institutions to offer you more (interest on your investments, or savings on your loans) to win your business.

❋ ❋ ❖ ❋ ❋ ❋ ❖ ❋ ❋ ❖ ❋ ❋ ❖ ❋ ❋ ❖ ❋ ❋ ❖ ❋ ❋ ❖ ❋ ❋ ❖ ❋ ❋ ❖ ❋ ❋

Be aware that with a variable-rate loan, if rates rise dramatically the monthly loan payment may not cover all of the interest since the payment was established based on interest rates in effect at the start of the loan. The interest not paid would still be owed, or you may be required to increase the monthly payment. If you choose a variable-rate loan, watch where interest rates are going and lock in when rates appear to be rising. The last thing you need is to get stuck with a loan with a variable rate going up, up, up!

What Is a Demand Loan?

This is a loan for which the lender can ask (demand) repayment at any time — referred to as "calling" the loan. However, a repayment schedule is usually established at the time the loan is granted. Payments on demand loans can be blended, fixed principal plus interest, or interest only. The interest charged usually floats.

Some people choose a "fixed principal plus interest payment" where a specified amount of principal plus the interest accrued is repaid each month. If you choose this method, the payments may not be a fixed amount each month because the interest charged may vary from month to month. Alternatively the financial institution may ask for additional payments to cover the increased interest amount if rates go up.

Connie Davis decided to buy a partnership in a commercial property venture. A demand loan was being offered by the institution that was financing the partnership deal. Connie decided she wanted to use a "fixed principal plus interest payment" so that she would have the loan paid off within five years. She chose to pay off $500 a month in principal plus whatever interest was owed. That means she would pay off $6,000 a year in principal, plus the interest. She began by making monthly payments of $725 a month. Since interest rates went up midway during the term, she eventually had to make payments of $825 a month to keep up.

With an interest-only loan, while the monthly interest costs must be paid each month, no principal is repaid. The principal remains outstanding for the full term of the loan, and interest is calculated on the full principal each month. Some people use this type of interest calculation when they are borrowing for investment purposes and want to minimize their cash flow outlay, particularly when they wish to use the interest paid as a tax deduction for income tax purposes.

Connie's husband, Dalton, also took a share in the same commercial property venture. Dalton chose to use an interest-only loan so that his cash flow wouldn't be strapped. His payments started out at $225 a month and eventually rose to $325 a month. However, he made no payments against his principal. At the end of five years, he still owed the total principal, while Connie had her loan completely paid off. However, since Dalton was doing considerably more investing than Connie, this suited his purposes. He knew exactly how much interest he had paid each month (for tax purposes) and he could easily work the $325 payments into his cash flow.

What Is a Personal Line of Credit?

A personal line of credit (PLC) is a floating-rate loan that establishes a specific amount of credit available to you. Since the maximum credit limit available is established when the PLC is approved, you don't have to be concerned with the delays or justification associated with applying for a new loan each time you need credit. Once approved, you have immediate access to the credit line established, and can use it whenever you like for whatever you like. You are often provided with a set of PLC cheques, which you can write to access the line. So, when you go to buy that new furniture, you can simply write a cheque and the money will come from the PLC to cover it.

A PLC is "revolving credit" or "open-ended credit," like a credit card. However, unlike a credit card, you can take advantage of interest rates that are often lower than those offered on instalment and demand loans. Interest on a PLC is usually calculated daily on the outstanding balance and charged monthly. The payment amount is not fixed, but a minimum monthly payment is required. Payments are applied against the outstanding balance with no prepayment penalty so you can make a full repayment at any time.

PLCs are usually offered to customers who have established a good credit history and have proven their ability to handle credit effectively. Not everyone can get one. Many financial institutions require that you have a minimum household income of $50,000 a year to qualify. That's because a PLC is a revolving line of credit and lenders are especially cautious. When a financial institution grants you a PLC, it's a vote of confidence in your ability to handle credit. And a PLC can be a tricky form of credit to manage. The line is easy to access and payment amounts are very flexible so the line can grow quickly. Some people get PLCs for the right reasons, but use them in ways that are not really to their best advantage.

Patsy has had a PLC for the past four years. She recently decided she wanted to buy a new car. Her sports car was still in great shape, but having just married, she wanted a car that could hold her newly acquired family. Her stepchildren were tired of trying to squeeze Into the nonexistent back seat, and her husband really hated the lack of leg room. Patsy ran an ad to sell her sports car, but there were no takers by the time she decided to buy her new car. She'd intended to use the proceeds from the sale of her car as a down payment and take out an instalment loan to finance the difference. Instead, she used her PLC to finance the down payment. She figured she'd pay off the balance when she sold the sports car. It would only be a couple of weeks.

After three months of making the lowest possible payments on her PLC, Patsy still hadn't sold her sports car and paid off the line. She hadn't even run another ad. Another three months passed and she decided she'd better run an ad. Six weeks later, the sports car sold for $12,600 and Patsy paid down the PLC. By then she had paid almost $924 in interest on the PLC.

PLC are useful for a number of reasons, but instant gratification shouldn't be one of them. It cost Patsy about $693 more than necessary to carry that PLC balance. You can buy a lot for $693. And that's all after-tax dollars. She would have to earn about $1,025 at her marginal tax rate to break even. There are good reasons to borrow, and not-so-good reasons to borrow.

To Borrow or Not to Borrow...

Many people fear getting into debt because of their upbringing or personal beliefs. The fact is that using credit is a part of life. Whether you are financing the purchase of new appliances, replacing your furnace or financing your children's education, borrowing can offer real benefits. After all, it'd be pretty tough on the family to have to to wait out a winter while you saved all the money you needed to buy a new furnace. Borrowing money, putting in the furnace and paying off the loan in easily manageable payments makes a lot more sense.

The question shouldn't simply be whether or not to borrow. Sometimes we have to.

Instead, ask yourself:

- Do I really need it?
- What's this going to cost me?
- What else do I have to give up to buy this?

If you need a furnace, my best guess is that your answer to the first question is a resounding *yes*.

The next question is a very important one. The cost of borrowing can vary significantly. The higher the interest rate you pay, the greater the cost. Also, the longer the term of the loan, the greater the cost to you. By negotiating the lowest possible rate and taking the shortest possible term, you can pay off the loan faster while reducing the overall costs.

But don't overlook the last question either. The more the payments restrict your cash flow, the greater the cost to you in terms of stress and having to go without other things you feel contribute to a comfortable lifestyle. If you choose to make higher payments over a shorter term, you have to be sure your other important living needs can still be met. Resist the urge to steal from Peter to pay Paul. Paying off your loan quickly won't do you any good if you run up your charge cards during the process. If you choose instead to take a slightly longer term so that your payments are lower and fit more comfortably into your cash flow, remember this will mean a longer commitment and more interest over the full term of the loan. Weigh the answers to each of these questions carefully in deciding how you'll manage your credit needs.

What Is a Secured PLC?

A PLC can either be secured or unsecured. That is, with or without collateral being offered as security for the loan. A secured PLC can mean significantly lower interest costs. When a PLC is secured with equity in your home, it is often referred to as a "home equity line of credit" (HELC) and sometimes as a "collateral mortgage." If you have equity in your home in excess of the current market value of the property less any outstanding debt, you can use that equity to secure your PLC. For example, if you have a home worth $170,000 and an outstanding mortgage of $100,000, you would have $70,000 in equity.

When you use your home to secure a PLC, the equity must usually equal a minimum of 30 percent. That means that outstanding debt registered on the property, including the PLC limit, cannot exceed 70 percent of the appraised value of the property.

Cathy and Roberto Brida have a home worth approximately $200,000 and an annual family income of $65,000. Their outstanding mortgage is $100,000. That means the Bridas would qualify for a home equity line of credit of $40,000:

70% of $200,000 = $140,000 less outstanding mortgage of $100,000 = $40,000

All about Security

With many personal loans, the only security required for the loan is your signature as a representation of your willingness to repay. However, in some circumstances lenders may require that security take the form of real estate, or investments such as stocks and bonds. When these types of assets are offered as security, they are referred to as collateral.

By offering collateral, you may be able to borrow more than you could simply on your signature. As well, it is also very likely that you will be able to borrow at a lower interest rate. The reason for this is that if you default, the lender can take possession of the collateral as payment toward the balance of the loan.

In order to benefit from the secured rate, loans must often be 100 percent secured. Real estate equity and investments such as Canada Savings Bonds, GICs or debentures, and mutual funds are often used as collateral. For collateral other than real estate, often referred to as "paper securities," only a percentage of the asset's value may be accepted as security. This is referred to as the "margin requirement." The amount you qualify to borrow will be based on the fair market value of the security — what it's worth when you're using it as collateral, not what you paid for it.

Margin requirements vary with the type of security being pledged and from one financial institution to another. For example, typically only 50 percent of the market value of stock is accepted as security for a loan. The reason is that the price of stocks can be volatile, increasing or decreasing very quickly. Since, typically, only 50 percent of their market value will be accepted as collateral, even significant decreases in value will not result in insufficient collateral to cover the loan.

Assets pledged as collateral are reviewed periodically, and if the value of the assets has decreased and there is not enough collateral to cover the loan, you will be asked to pledge additional assets to secure the loan.

In legal terms, most movable property such as cars, boats and trailers are referred to as chattels. When you use this type of property to secure a loan, you are often required to sign a promissory note and a chattel mortgage giving the lender the right to take possession of the property if you default on the loan. Most car loans are actually chattel mortgages with the car being used as security for the loan.

A chattel mortgage contains a number of conditions that you must meet. For example, you cannot use the same property as security for any other loan or PLC, the property cannot be sold without the permission of the lender, nor can the property be removed from the jurisdiction outlined by the lender.

What Is Overdraft Protection?

Overdraft protection is often not thought of as a form of credit. Many people see overdraft protection as a convenience for which they pay dearly. In fact, just like a PLC and a credit card, overdraft protection is a revolving line of credit. Typically used to meet shortages in cash flow, overdrafts charge significantly higher rates of interest than other forms of credit (except of course credit cards). For a hefty price, you never have to be concerned about the costs and embarrassment associated with NSF (non-sufficient funds) cheques.

The impact of an NSF cheque is "bigger" than the costs associated.

Donovan wasn't particularly good at managing his accounts. Between his mortgage payment, his car loan and making all the other regular household payments each month, he kept running short just when he needed cash most. Three or four times this year, he wrote cheques without enough money in his account to cover them. The cheques were returned NSF and Donovan paid substantial NSF fees. And each time he wrote an NSF cheque, it was reported on his credit history file.

The real cost of those NSF cheques finally came back to haunt Donovan when he went to a bank to apply for a loan to replace his roof. The lender took a look at his NSF cheque history and declined Donovan's request. From the lender's perspective, Donovan's bad habit demonstrated his inability to handle his finances and meet his commitments. Donovan applied to another bank, and after a long and drawn-out discussion was given the loan. But Donovan ended up paying 2.5 percent more in interest because of his bad credit history.

If you find you tend to run short of cash partway through the month, you might consider using overdraft protection as a way of avoiding NSF cheques. From a sound credit management perspective, the best way to avoid problems and the need for overdraft protection is to spend only what you have available. However, from time to time, many people find themselves in a cash flow squeeze. You can use overdraft protection to ensure that squeeze doesn't have a long-term negative impact on your credit rating.

A Word about Store Financing

Sometimes when people think they won't qualify for a bank loan, they decide to take advantage of store financing. Sometimes store financing looks so attractive, it seems like the best deal going. You've seen those ads that say, "Pay nothing down and make no payments till..." Well, here's what happens if you can't pay off your purchase on time.

Sometimes the store where you bought the item has its own credit financing. When it does, the interest paid is often tied to the store's credit card rate. That means you'll be charged the same rate as you would have been if you'd put the purchase on your credit card. While in October 1992, financial institutions were charging between eight and 10.5 percent annually for a loan, a store credit card was charging 2.4 percent *a month*, or 28 percent annually. That's a *big* difference.

Sometimes the store where you bought an item does the financing through a third party. This company takes over your debt, you make your payments directly to them and they charge you a financing cost. One company surveyed was charging 2.233 percent a month in October 1992. That's 26.79 percent a year.

Sally and Frank each bought $1,000 worth of furniture on a "pay nothing down" plan. Six months later when it came time to pay off the furniture, neither Sally or Frank had all the cash they needed to pay off the furniture. The finance company not only was charging 2.233 percent a month, it was also charging a one-time administration fee of $22.50. What was more interesting was how the interest on their balances was calculated.

Frank could come up with $600 toward the furniture so he only had to finance $400. Since he was paying off more than half of the original principal, the finance company calculated the interest on the $400 outstanding.

Sally, on the other hand, could only come up with $200. Since she was not making a minimum payment of 50 percent, the finance company charged her interest on the total balance of $1,000.

It's all in the paperwork you sign when you buy the item. Make sure you read it carefully before you sign on the dotted line. The last thing you need is to find out, too late, that the financing you agreed to will cost more than you thought.

At that point you might think that all you have to do is get a bank loan to pay off the furniture. It may not be as easy, or as inexpensive, as you think. Often financial institutions tie the money they lend to the purpose of the loan. If you want a loan to pay off a furniture purchase, the financial institution may charge you its credit card rate of interest. (In October 1992, that was about 17 percent.) Why? Simple. They don't want you to use a loan for a purchase you could make on your credit card. They don't want the hassle of going through all the paperwork and procedures for what they consider to be a small loan. Instead, they would rather you used your credit card. So they charge you the same rate of interest to dissuade you from using their loans to finance such small purchases.

Not all financial institutions make their decisions strictly on the basis of purpose. Shop around. There are companies that base their decisions on you, your credit history, and your worth to them as a customer. Find a lender who treats you like a person and recognizes your individual needs. Then give him your business. Remember, you're the customer. You have rights, and one is the right not to pay outrageously high interest. Shop around. Be discriminating. Make your decision based on the following:

- Is it the best deal going?
- Is the price negotiable?
- Does this lender deserve my business?

Choosing the Right Type of Credit for Your Needs

The type of loan you choose will depend on:

- its purpose
- where interest rates are — and where they're going
- your cash flow requirements
- your ability to qualify

The purpose of the loan will have an effect on which type of loan you choose. If you're financing the purchase of a car, an instalment loan may be your best bet. If, on the other hand, you need access to an ongoing source of credit to use for investment purposes, a PLC may be just the ticket.

Where interest rates are and where they are going also have an impact on the loan you choose. If rates are rising and you choose a variable-rate instalment loan, a demand loan or a PLC/HELC, then the interest you pay will rise too. However, if you choose a fixed-rate instalment loan, you can lock in the current rate for the term chosen. Of course, the opposite is true in periods when interest rates are falling. Then you may wish a loan with a fluctuating rate of interest so you can pay less interest as rates fall.

Also consider how the loan repayment amount affects your overall cash flow. If you want a loan that charges interest only so you can minimize the impact on your cash flow, a demand loan may be the answer. If you want a loan that allows you to make minimum payments, a PLC/HELC can do just that for you. If you are looking for a guaranteed, fixed payment amount for the full term so you can budget accurately, a fixed-rate instalment loan is the answer. If you need an option that lets you make your repayments more often than once a month (i.e., weekly, bi-weekly or semi-monthly) to fit in with how often you are paid, an instalment loan likely meets that need.

Whether or not you qualify is also part of the decision-making. For example, while most instalment and demand loans have no minimum household-income requirements, many financial institutions require that you have a minimum household income of $50,000 a year to qualify for a PLC.

As you can see, there is a wide range of options from which to choose if you need to borrow money. Knowing what you want is the first step. The second step is being flexible so that you can take advantage of any advice offered by the lender. Remember, you're in this together. You need the money to meet your immediate needs. The lender wants to be sure you'll repay the loan in full and on time. Working together, you can both achieve your objectives.

❋ ❋

If you think you're paying more interest on a loan that you should be, try to refinance the loan. Perhaps rates have fallen since you originally took the loan. Maybe you didn't shop around enough the first time.

Many loans allow full repayment at any time. Have a chat with your lender and discuss how you can reduce your interest costs. Assuming everything goes smoothly, with a lower interest rate, your monthly payments will also be lower. But don't take a lower monthly payment. By keeping your payment amount the same, you'll have your loan paid off more quickly.

If you can't get any satisfaction at your current financial institution, shop around. When you find a lower rate, let your lender know. If the lender matches the rate, great. If not, take your business elsewhere. After all, lenders are just selling money, and there are lots of places to buy it. Remember, *you're* the customer.

3 Mortgages

Whether you are buying your first house, trading up to a larger home or building your dream home, a house is likely to be the single largest investment you will ever make. Since almost everyone who is purchasing a home will require financial assistance, you have to plan carefully to ensure everything goes smoothly.

The first things most people want to know is how much they can afford to spend and what their mortgage payments will be. But there are all sorts of other questions that need answers. First-time buyers often need guidance on what to look for in a mortgage. Most people want to know how they can pay the least amount of interest over the term of their mortgage. Some people are concerned about protecting their investment. Some people want to know exactly what a mortgage is.

What Is a Mortgage?

It's something you can't live without — not if you ever want to own your own home. The word "mortgage" — (mort = death) + (gage = pledge of commitment) — even suggests how folks in the olden days saw mortgages: as a commitment till death. Back then, the mortgage-burning party was a wonderful celebration of freedom. I'm happy to say that many of us no longer see our mortgages as everlasting. Many of us can see the light at the end of the tunnel — and most of us go right back out and dig a bigger hole for ourselves, just as daylight is around the corner.

In financial terms, a mortgage is a loan that uses a property, such as a house or condominium, as security to ensure the debt is repaid. The borrower is referred to as the mortgagor, the lender as the mortgagee. The actual amount of the loan is referred to as the principal, and the mortgagor is expected to repay that principal, along with interest, over the repayment period (amortization) of the mortgage.

Are Mortgages Only Used for Buying Homes?

Actually, you can use a mortgage for financing lots of things, including:

- purchasing or constructing a new home
- purchasing an existing home
- financing a renovation
- consolidating debts
- acquiring other assets

Since a mortgage is a fully secured form of financing, the interest you pay is usually considerably less than with most other types of financing. The only thing that comes close is a secured PLC.

Andy and Elizabeth Tuner have just bought a new home. The house is in the older part of the city, and Elizabeth wants to renovate the kitchen and bathrooms. When the Tuners applied for their mortgage, they applied for an additional $28,000 above what they needed to finance the purchase in order to make those renovations.

Andy's sister, Vicky, and her husband are living in a home in the same area where the Tuners have bought. Vicky and her husband, Mark McLean, are planning to refinance their mortgage when it comes due in June. With two children in university, the McLeans have had to take a couple of loans over the past two years to finance residence fees and tuition. Now, with the mortgage up for renewal, they have decided to consolidate all their debts using a single mortgage. Since their loans are at 11.5% and the current five-year mortgage rate is only 8.75%, they know they will be saving considerably on the cost of their financing.

 Some people choose to use the equity in their homes to finance the purchase of investments. Using either a secured PLC or a mortgage, they can benefit from the lower costs, and they can write off the interest costs against their taxable incomes.

This is also the only way to make your mortgage interest tax deductible.

Let's say your $90,000 mortgage is coming up for renewal. Let's also say that you need $10,000 in cash to invest. If you take out a mortgage of $100,000 and use $10,000 for investments, you would be able to write off the interest costs associated with that $10,000.

Polly and Geoffrey used this concept with a slightly different twist. Geoff had been transferred to Edmonton and they decided not to sell their existing home in Toronto. The real estate market had fallen off significantly, and they thought it best to wait until they were sure everything worked out in Edmonton before selling the house.

Polly and Geoff decided to rent the house in Toronto, thus making it an investment property. This meant they could write off the mortgage interest costs against the income generated from the rental. However, the mortgage on the Toronto house was almost completely paid off. Polly and Geoff decided to increase the mortgage and use that money as a down payment on their new house in Edmonton.

Types of Mortgages

The type of mortgage you qualify for will depend on the amount of your down payment. If your down payment is 25 percent or more, you will likely qualify for a conventional mortgage. However, if your down payment is between 10 and 25 percent, then a high-ratio mortgage will provide the financing you need to buy your home.

> Darrian and Donna Devereau have found the perfect home. Priced at $172,000, the Devereaus have a down payment of $44,000 (or 25.58%) — enough to qualify for a conventional mortgage.

> Jerry and Julia Jackson have also decided to buy a new home. It, too, is valued at $172,000. However, the Jacksons have a down payment of $20,000 (or 11.62%). While they won't qualify for a conventional mortgage, the Jacksons can still finance their home purchase using a high-ratio mortgage.

A conventional mortgage is a loan that does not exceed 75 percent of the appraised value or purchase price of the property, whichever is less. A high-ratio mortgage is a loan that exceeds 75 percent (but usually no more than 90 percent) of the appraised value or purchase price of the property, whichever is less. These loans are granted under the provisions of the National Housing Act (NHA) of 1954 and are sometimes referred to as NHA-insured mortgages. High-ratio mortgages must be insured against loss by the Canada Mortgage and Housing Corporation (CMHC) or the Mortgage Insurance Corporation of Canada (MICC).

❋ ❋

In 1992, CMHC and MICC introduced a special program called the First Home Loan Insurance program, designed to assist first-time home buyers. Under this plan, your minimum down payment can be as low as five percent. This means if you're eligible, you can get financing for up to 95 percent of the sale price, the appraised value or the maximum house price, whichever is least.

To be eligible, you must buy a home in Canada, with the intention of occupying that home as your principal residence, and you cannot have owned a principal residence during the previous five years.

If you and your spouse (or you and a friend) are applying jointly (i.e., there is more than one applicant), only one of you needs to meet these eligibility requirements.

You will be asked to complete and sign a certification of eligibility, and this certification is sent to CMHC/MICC along with the other application documents.

The term of the mortgage must be five years. Minimum house prices have been established across the country for eligibility under this program, and the program is currently slated to run until 1994.

❋ ❋

What's the Difference between a First Mortgage and a Second Mortgage?

A first mortgage is a debt registered against a property that is secured by a first "charge," or "call," on the property. That means if you default (i.e., you don't make the required payment[s]), the first lender has first right on the value of the property in order to recover the principal and any outstanding interest plus costs.

A second mortgage comes next in line. In most cases, the interest charged on a second mortgage is higher, reflecting the increased risk to the lender.

What's the Difference between an Open Mortgage and a Closed Mortgage?

If you want the flexibility to repay your mortgage whenever you wish, without penalty, you may want to look at an open mortgage.

It allows you to repay the loan on any payment date without penalty, and usually has a shorter term (six months or one year) with a higher interest rate than available with a closed mortgage.

If you want the security of fixed payments or wish long-term financing, choose a closed mortgage. A closed mortgage cannot be prepaid or renegotiated, and if extra payments are made, a prepayment penalty may be charged, depending on the specific terms of the mortgage. Terms for closed mortgages can range from six months to as long as 15 years, though most financial institutions offer one- to five-year terms.

Fixed- versus Variable-Rate Mortgages

With a fixed-rate mortgage, the interest rate is set for the term of the mortgage so that the monthly payment of principal and interest remains the same throughout the term. Regardless of whether rates move up or down, you know exactly how much interest you will be paying and what your payment amounts will be. Therefore a fixed-rate mortgage provides protection from fluctuations in interest rates and simplifies your personal budgeting.

A variable-rate (also called floating- or adjustable-rate) mortgage provides you with maximum flexibility during times of fluctuating interest rates since the rate is based on prime and can be adjusted monthly to reflect current rates. Typically, the mortgage payment remains constant, but the ratio between interest and principal fluctuates. When interest rates are falling, you pay less interest and more principal. If rates are rising, the interest component will also rise, and less of your payment will go toward the principal. As with a variable-rate loan, you should be aware that if rates rise dramatically, the original payment amount may not cover both the principal and interest components of the mortgage. The interest not paid is still owed, or you may be asked to increase your monthly payment. Some companies have variable-rate mortgages that are automatically open or convertible to a fixed-rate mortgage. That way, if rates begin to rise you can lock in your rate for a specific term.

What's the Difference between the Amortization and the Term?

When deciding how to structure your mortgage, one of the things to consider is your cash flow. The amount you can afford to repay each month will have an impact on the amortization and term you choose.

Amortization refers to the number of years it will take to repay the entire amount of the mortgage based on a set of fixed payments. For example, if a $100,000 mortgage is amortized at 10 percent over 10 years, the monthly payments would be $1,310.34. For the same mortgage amortized over 25 years, the monthly payments would be only $894.49.

The longer the amortization chosen, the smaller the monthly payment, but the more interest paid over the life of the mortgage. Some people choose a long amortization schedule to lower their monthly payments to meet their cash flow needs. Others choose a short amortization schedule to reduce the amount of interest they have to pay.

While "amortization" refers to the number of years it will take to repay the entire loan, the "term" of the mortgage is the amount of time that the mortgage agreement covers, usually anywhere from six months to 15 years.

Choosing the term of your mortgage requires a bit of crystal-gazing. You should choose the term of your mortgage based on how you think interest rates will change over time. If you feel interest rates are low and you want to take advantage of those low rates for as long as possible, choose a fixed-rate mortgage for as long a term as you can get. If you think rates may be falling, choose a one-year open mortgage, a variable-rate mortgage, or a fixed six-month term and renew at the lower interest rate when the term expires.

Figuring Out What You Can Afford

There are two things you have to think about when you decide you want to buy property:

- How much can you afford to spend?
- How large a mortgage payment can you handle?

A starting point in figuring out how much you can afford is to multiply your gross annual income (your income before taxes) by 2.5. Include only income you're sure you will receive, and if you and your spouse both have incomes, add them together (referred to as your household income).

> Thomas and Laura want to buy their first house. Thomas has been working for a major appliance manufacturer for the past four years. He has a gross salary of $32,000. Sometimes he receives an annual bonus of $2,000 to $3,000 when the company does particularly well. Laura works for a dry-cleaning company in the marketing department and makes $26,000 a year gross.
>
> Since they should only use the income of which they are sure, Thomas and Laura leave out Thomas's potential bonus. Here's how their calculation works:
>
> $32,000 + $26,000 = $58,000 x 2.5 = $145,000

Based on this calculation, Thomas and Laura could afford to buy a house with a price tag of $145,000 or less. Remember, however, this is only an *estimate*.

FIGURING OUT WHAT YOU CAN AFFORD

YOUR GROSS HOUSEHOLD INCOME   \$_____

MULTIPLIED BY 2.5   \$_____

EQUALS YOUR ESTIMATED PURCHASE PRICE   \$_____

MONTHLY EXPENSES

GROCERIES   \$_____

CLOTHING   \$_____

TRANSPORTATION   \$_____

ENTERTAINMENT   \$_____

EXISTING CREDIT PAYMENTS   \$_____

MEDICAL & DENTAL   \$_____

PERSONAL (E.G., GIFTS, HAIRCUTS, COSMETICS)   \$_____

INSURANCE   \$_____

RRSP CONTRIBUTIONS   \$__•_____

SAVINGS   \$_____

OTHER   \$_____

YOUR TOTAL MONTHLY EXPENSES   \$_____

YOUR NET MONTHLY HOUSEHOLD INCOME   \$_____

LESS YOUR TOTAL MONTHLY EXPENSES   \$_____

LESS ESTIMATED HOUSE MAINTENANCE
(ESTIMATED PURCHASE PRICE X 0.5%)   \$_____

EQUALS YOUR ESTIMATED MANAGEABLE
MORTGAGE PAYMENT AMOUNT   \$_____

*Did you remember to include all your expenses, even those
not paid for monthly such as your car insurance and your vet bills?
Did you remember to feed the cat?
Did you include what you spend for newspapers, coffee and lunch each day?
If you're a little over your head, where can you reasonably cut back
on your expenses?
Did you remember to include a savings account for emergencies?*

Of course, not only do you have to think about the price of house you can afford, you must also consider how you will work those mortgage payments into your monthly budget. The general rule is that you can usually afford a payment in the range of 20 to 30 percent of your gross monthly income. This should also include the cost of the property taxes.

> If Thomas and Laura's total monthly income is $4,833.33, then based on this guideline, they would be able to afford a monthly payment between $966 and $1,450 for their mortgage and property taxes combined.

Of course, the amount Thomas and Laura can actually afford to spend each month will also depend on whether they have other debts, such as a car loan, credit card balances or a student loan. As well, the amount they spend on items such as clothing, transportation, food, entertainment and so on would also have to be considered. Since Thomas was married before and has a four-year-old for whom he pays support, this would also have to be taken into account.

In figuring out how much you can afford, the best thing to do is to add up how much you spend, except for housing, and deduct the total from your monthly take-home pay. Then consider carefully what it will cost to live in your new home. Ask friends or family who live in a home similar to what you're looking for what their heating, electricity, water, insurance, repair and maintenance bills are like.

I remember when I bought my first home, I made no allowance for a lawn mower. My poor brother used to come once a month at nine o'clock at night to cut my lawn (using my parents' mower since he didn't have one either). The yard looked good one week a month and the neighbours hated me!

Pre-Approval

The safest way to find out exactly how much you can afford to spend and what your payments will be is to get pre-approved. To do so, you go to a financial institution and a lender will work out all the figures to tell you how much you will probably be able to afford to spend on a house, and how much your monthly mortgage payments will be.

When interest rates are rising, most people also want some way of protecting their interest rate until they find a home. Most pre-approvals offer an interest rate guarantee for anywhere from 30 to 90 days. To get the guaranteed rate, you must complete the transaction (i.e., close the house and have the mortgage funds disbursed) within the guaranteed period. If the period expires, the guarantee is gone.

When interest rates are lower at closing than the rate guaranteed, the financial institution will usually provide the mortgage at the lower rate. You can have the peace of mind of knowing your interest rate is protected, particularly when interest rates are fluctuating.

A pre-approval also produces an offer to purchase that may be more attractive to the seller, who may weigh the fact that you have pre-approved financing in your favour. But just because you have a pre-approved mortgage doesn't mean you're guaranteed the financing. You should still make your offer conditional on financing. Your pre-approval is based on your credit worthiness, down payment and ability to service the debt. However, since you haven't chosen the house you're going to buy yet, the mortgage is only approved in principle. Final approval is subject to the property qualifying. An appraisal is needed to determine this. Once you have located the house you want to buy, the normal mortgage application procedure is followed. However, since much of the preliminary qualifying information has already been obtained, your application can usually be handled much more quickly.

Just because you've been pre-approved by one lender doesn't mean you have to borrow from them. You can still shop around. Another financial institution may offer a feature you find particularly attractive.

Don't fall into the trap of not shopping around simply because it is easier to be pre-approved by your existing financial institution. Times they are a'changin', and financial institutions are always trying to come up with new ways to lure you into their stores. Make sure you know what you want, and shop till you find it.

The Closing Process

- You apply for financing and the financial institution does its thing to grant you the mortgage, including the credit investigation. (See chapter 4.)

- You will be asked to sign a letter of commitment.

- You provide your lawyer with the Agreement of Purchase and Sale, and he or she does preliminary searches (on title, property taxes, utilities such as hydro and gas, zoning, executions on vendor, etc.).

- Your financial institution sends Instructions to Solicitor forms to your lawyer, and your lawyer talks to the vendor's (house-seller's) lawyer to ensure title is clear and required declarations are made.

- At closing, your financial institution transfers funds to your lawyer's trust account. Your lawyer does the final searches at the registry office and meets with the vendor's lawyer at the land registry office to exchange documents (the deed and other declarations, the house keys and cheques).

- Your lawyer registers the deed and mortgage on title at the registry office and prepares a reporting letter to both you and your financial institution.

For people who are selling one house and buying another, the process is more complicated because they must also discharge (or port) their mortgage. For people who need CMHC/MICC insurance, there are additional steps to follow. The application must be forwarded to CMHC/MICC for their approval and undertaking to insure the mortgage.

Preparing for the Mortgage Interview

When applying for a mortgage, you have to provide specific information about your financial circumstances. Take the following documentation with you when meeting to apply for a mortgage:

- personal identification such as your driver's licence or social insurance card, as well as a list of personal information, including your address, the name of your landlord or present

45

mortgage holder, and the amount you are now paying in rent or for your mortgage.

- a list of all your assets and liabilities with a realistic value set for each; also a list of all your credit cards, as you'll probably be asked for the numbers (to check your credit history).

- written confirmation of employment income from your employer, and confirmation in writing of income from any other sources, showing a consistent amount from year to year; you might want to take your notices of assessment from Revenue Canada as proof of your income history

- for self-employed people, the last three years' income tax returns and/or financial statements.

- a copy of the accepted purchase agreement, along with a statement regarding urea formaldehyde foam insulation (this statement is normally included on the standard offer of purchase forms used by real estate brokers) and a photograph of the house or a copy of the listing.

- your lawyer's name, full address and telephone number.

- who to contact for access to the property for the appraisal (the person's name, full address and telephone number) — may be the realtor or the vendor.

- heating cost estimate and property tax estimate (usually found on the listing) and condominium fees, if applicable.

- for properties that do not have municipal services, well and/or septic tank certificates.

- confirmation of down payment. This is also required in cases when your down payment is coming from sources other than your own savings or investments. If it is a gift, a letter confirming that *it is a gift with no repayment terms* is needed. If the down payment is to come from a second mortgage, a written confirmation of the terms and conditions of this mortgage must be provided by the second mortgagor.

Choosing a Term You Can Live With

What term should you take? Well…that's a good question. Before you look at the issue of term specifically, there are things you should consider to manage your mortgage to your best advantage.

When you're looking at term and interest rates, look also at what you can live with in terms of payment amounts and amortization. There's a direct relation between the interest rate, payment amount and amortization period.

If, for example, you take a $100,000 mortgage at 10 percent with a 20-year amortization period, your monthly payment would be $951.67. If the rates go up, say to 11 percent, your monthly payment would also go up to $1,015.64. However if rates fall to, say, nine percent, your monthly payment would also fall to $889.19. So the lower your interest rate, the lower your payment amount.

Now let's look at how the amortization period affects your payment. With a $100,000 mortgage at 10 percent with a 20-year amortization period, we said your monthly payments would be $951.67. If you choose a 25-year amortization period, your payments would only be $894.49. With a 15-year amortization period, your payment would rise to $1,062.27. So the longer your amortization, the lower your payment amount, and the shorter the amortization period, the higher your payment amount.

Now, putting these two factors together will help you to figure out what you can live with. The first place to start is to figure out the payment amount with which you'll be comfortable over the long term. Since interest rates are beyond your control, you only have the option of playing with the amortization period to get the payment amount you want.

Okay, so you've decided on the amortization that will give you the payment amount you want. Now you have to consider what will happen if rates go up or down. Since the "up" is the one we all hate, let's look at it first.

If rates go up, you have two choices. First, you can work the increased payment amount into your budget. Second, you can increase your amortization to bring your payment amount back in line. Now, that may mean moving your mortgage to another financial institution, so be prepared for the cost of writing a new mortgage.

What if rates go down? Great! Now you could benefit from a lower payment amount. But think about this a minute. You've already worked the payment into your budget. If you keep your payment amount the same, you'll be paying off your mortgage a lot faster. So, don't pocket the difference. Keep applying it to your mortgage .

One final point on managing your mortgage. Rather than locking yourself into a high payment amount that you have to struggle to make each month, do yourself a favour. If you don't *have* to put yourself in this position, choose a payment amount you find easier to live with. Then make sure you have prepayment options that allow you to make additional payments against your mortgage when you have the cash available. That way, you'll have a payment amount you can manage comfortably, and you can still aggressively pay down your mortgage.

Now, back to the term. You still have to decide what term is best for you. Here are some questions to ask yourself:

• Where are rates now and where are they going?

Trying to predict where rates are going is a tough job. You can twist yourself into knots worrying about what will happen. At the end of 1992, we saw interest rates fall to their lowest in 35 years. No one ever thought they'd get that low again. Wrong! Equally wrong is to assume that rates can't skyrocket again. I know it's bad economics, but if anyone had told us in the 70s that interest rates would be in the upper teens in the 80s we'd have said they were crazy.

If you feel rates are at a point you can live with and you want to guarantee that rate for as long as possible, you'd choose a long term, referred to as "going long." This is also true if rates appear to be rising and you want to take advantage of the lower rate for as long as possible.

But what if rates are falling? If so, you may want to give yourself the flexibility to take advantage of the lower rates. You can do that in a number of ways. You can choose a short term — "going short" — or an open mortgage for which you'll pay a higher rate of interest. You can choose a variable-rate mortgage so that as rates come down you benefit from the lower rate. Or you can choose a convertible mortgage, which lets you take advantage of lower rates and then lock in a rate if you feel the rates have bottomed out and will start to rise.

• Do you want a fixed payment amount?

Some people choose a long-term mortgage to ensure they'll have a fixed payment amount they can live with for as long as possible. This makes it much easier to budget your mortgage payments and everything else in your life — particularly when you're budgeting to your last red cent and even a small upward movement in interest rates would be extremely hard on your cash flow.

- Are you a gambler?

Some people don't mind the stomach turning associated with fluctuations in rates. Others can't stand the stress. If you're not comfortable with the gambling game, pick a payment amount you can live with and lock it in for the mid- to long-term (three to five years).

- Are you prepared to keep a close eye on the market?

If you're going to choose a short term or an open, variable-rate or convertible mortgage, then you're going to have to keep a careful watch on what interest rates are doing so you can lock in when rates bottom out. If you're not prepared to do this, then go with a mid- to long-term rate and hope for the best.

Payment Frequencies

Once you know how much you can afford to spend, you have to decide how often you want to make your payments. With constant demands on their cash flows, most people want a way of maintaining control over the payment of their mortgages. Most financial institutions provide you with a choice of payment frequencies for all fixed-rate mortgages so that you can choose when and how often you wish to make your regular payments.

You can choose from:

1. Monthly (12 payments/year)
2. Semi-Monthly (24 payments/year)
3. Bi-weekly (26 payments/year)
4. Weekly (52 payments/year)
5. "Faster-pay" bi-weekly (26 payments/year)
6. "Faster-pay" weekly (52 payments/year)

The first four alternatives are ways to make payments fit conveniently with your cash flow. The faster-pay alternatives allow you to make extra payments against your principal as part of your regular payment stream, in order to save on interest and reduce the amortization of your mortgage.

If you want the ease and convenience of one fixed monthly payment amount, the amount is calculated using the amortization tables available in libraries and most bookstores.

If you are paid semi-monthly, you may wish to use a semi-monthly frequency to match your cash flow. Semi-monthly payments are calculated by taking the total annual mortgage payments and dividing by 24 (12 months x 2 payments a month). If you are paid bi-weekly, you may want to use a bi-weekly frequency. Bi-weekly payments are calculated by taking the total annual mortgage payments and dividing by 26 (52 weeks ÷ 2). Sometimes people choose to use a weekly frequency so smaller amounts are paid on a steady basis. Weekly payments are calculated by taking the total annual mortgage payments and dividing by 52.

Some people want to take advantage of the savings available by using a faster-pay or accelerated frequency. With this, you actually make extra payments against your mortgage, but do so in such small amounts that those extra payments can easily fit into your cash flow. With the faster-pay bi-weekly frequency, instead of dividing the total annual payment amount by 26, it is divided by 24 (as if the payments were being made on a semi-monthly frequency). However, you still make 26 payments during the year. So, if your monthly mortgage payment (from the amortization tables) is $1,000 and you use a bi-weekly frequency, your payments would be $461.54:

$$\frac{\$1,000 \times 12}{26} = \qquad \$461.54 \times 26 = \qquad \$12,000$$

However, if you choose a faster-pay bi-weekly frequency, your payments would be $500 and you would make one extra monthly payment for a total of $13,000 a year:

$$\frac{\$1,000 \times 12}{24} = \quad \$500 \times 26 \quad = \quad \$13,000$$

By making faster-pay bi-weekly payments, you actually make two extra payments a year (which translates into 13 monthly payments instead of 12). Those extra payments reduce your principal, so you save on your interest costs in the long term.

Faster-pay weekly payments work in much the same way. With this frequency, instead of dividing the total annual payment amount by 52, it is divided by 48 (as if the payments were being made on a monthly basis divided by four weeks). However, you still make 52 payments during the year. For example:

Weekly:

$$\frac{\$1,000 \times 12}{52} = \quad \$230.77 \times 52 \quad = \quad \$12,000$$

Faster-pay weekly:

$$\frac{\$1,000 \times 12}{12 \times 4} = \quad \$250.00 \times 52 \quad = \quad \$13,000$$

Based on a mortgage of $100,000 at a rate of 11 percent amortized over 25 years, you would realize a savings of $62,486 in interest over the life of the mortgage using a faster-pay weekly frequency.

How would you feel if someone offered to save you $62,486? Pretty good. And all you have to do is choose the faster-pay weekly frequency. It's easy, it's convenient and it saves money.

Many financial institutions allow you to change your payment frequency as your needs change. However, you should be aware that an interest adjustment charge from your current payment due date to the revised date may be required.

Making Payments

Typically, you can make your mortgage payments using an automatic debit plan in which the payment is automatically taken from your chequing account and applied to your mortgage. Using this option, you don't have to be concerned about writing a cheque, going into the branch or postal delays. Payments can be taken automatically from any account you choose, at any financial institution. Some financial institutions still accept postdated cheques, but this is becoming less and less popular. The administration involved in posting cheques individually (as opposed to an automatic system) means some institutions no longer offer this option.

An institution may try to insist that you open a chequing account at their branch to make your mortgage payments more convenient. Unless you intend to move your chequing account permanently, don't be persuaded. If you do, you'll find yourself running to the branch to make the deposit in time for the mortgage payment to be withdrawn. This is hardly convenient. If the lender gets pushy, push back. After all, it's your mortgage and there are lots of lenders who would like to get your business.

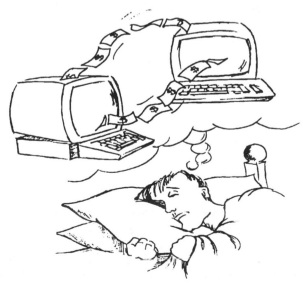

More about Making Extra Payments against Your Principal

Many financial institutions now offer mortgagees the flexibility to make extra payments against their mortgage principals without penalty. This is one of the most important features to look for when shopping for a mortgage. Here are some of the variations offered and how you can benefit:

- Make an additional payment a maximum of 12 times a year (or once a month) up to your normal payment amount. If, for example, your regular monthly payment amount is $1,200, you can make an additional $1,200 payment every month that will go directly to your principal. This will pay off your mortgage faster than you can believe. Just one extra monthly payment a year can significantly reduce the amortization and total interest cost on your mortgage.

- Increase your regular payment amount by up to double the original amount. So, if your regular monthly payment was $1,200, you could increase it to as much as $2,400. That means if you get a $100-a-month raise and want to increase your mortgage payment by $50, you can. Again, the extra amount paid goes directly toward your principal and can save you bags of money. The only drawback with this alternative is that with some financial institutions, once you raise your repayment amount, you can't go back.

- Make lump-sum payments of anywhere between 10 and 15 percent of your original principal once a year (with some institutions, on your anniversary date; with others, on any payment date).

Simone Dorrester has a $100,000 mortgage amortized over 25 years. If the interest rate on Simone's mortgage remains constant at 11 percent, with prepayments of as little as $1,000 once a year, she can save up to $57,533 in interest over the life of her mortgage, paying off the principal six and a half years sooner.

❀ ❀

If you have a high-interest mortgage and interest rates have fallen considerably, you may want to consider borrowing the money to make a principal prepayment. In effect, you'll be using less expensive debt (the loan) to pay down your more expensive debt (the mortgage). If you pledge assets to secure the loan, you should be able to get an even lower rate of interest on the loan. Alternatively, you may want to take a second mortgage, but remember to factor in the fees associated with writing a new mortgage.

Most financial institutions have software programs that can show you how much interest you'll save on your mortgage over the long term if you make a principal prepayment. Ask for a printout and then compare the interest savings with the cost of the loan/second mortgage. Do it if the dollar savings make sense and you can work the new loan/mortgage payment into your cash flow comfortably.

❀ ❀

- At least one financial institution I know of offers you the option of skipping a payment for every extra full monthly payment you make toward your mortgage during a single term. For example, if in June, July and August you made an extra full mortgage payment, you would then have the right to skip making payments in any three months up until the end of the term of the mortgage. Naturally, this doesn't pay your mortgage off much faster, but in times of economic constraint — such as in January when the Christmas bills are coming in, or if you're temporarily out of work — this can give you a little extra breathing room. You don't have to use the skips, but it's nice to know they are there if you need them. If you're self-employed, you might take a good hard look at this option. It may be just what you need to help even out your cash flow bumps. Make an extra payment when you have the money. Skip when you don't. The same applies to people who are financing rental property. If the property sits empty for a couple of months, but you've made extra payments during your term, you won't be strapped — you can just skip.

Prepayment options vary from one financial institution to another. Let your fingers do the walking and shop aggressively for the features you want.

If you wish to make additional lump sum payments in excess of those allowed as pre-payments by your financial institution, or if you wish to fully discharge (pay off) your mortgage, you can usually do so subject to a prepayment penalty.

What Is a Prepayment Penalty?

When you take out a mortgage with a financial institution, you make an agreement to pay the price (the interest) for using their money. If you decide to make a large prepayment (above that allowed under the terms of your mortgage) or renew your mortgage early, you have to compensate the financial institution for the interest you would have paid. This is sometimes referred to as a lost interest penalty, lost interest compensation (LIC) or interest rate differential (IRD). This is necessary because of a banking system called "matching."

When a bank receives a term deposit investment, say for five years, it knows it has that money available to lend for five years. When you take your mortgage for five years, the bank matches that money with your five-year term and, ta-dah! — a match made in heaven, or at least on a computer. If rates go down and you want to take advantage of the lower rates by renewing early, you have to compensate the financial institution for the money it would have made if you'd held the mortgage for the full term.

If it was your $50,000 on deposit for five years at 12 percent, would you put up with the financial institution's telling you it had changed its mind and decided to give you back your money and not pay you 12 percent when you know you can only get eight percent anywhere else? Nosiree! And financial institutions won't put up with it either. So they make you pay a penalty to recapture the interest they will lose when you renew early.

It can be pretty hard to take when you're actually in that position, but the fact remains you made a deal with the financial institution, and a deal is a deal. If you're still determined to prepay your mortgage or renew early, then bite the bullet and pay the lost interest compensation.

Now if it happens that your mortgage rate is lower than the current mortgage rate, the financial institution may still want to charge you a penalty. If you think about this, though, there wouldn't be any lost interest for the financial institution, because it could take the money you are prepaying (or paying back in full) and lend it to someone else at a higher rate. They'd actually make money on your decision. Sure, there'd be some administrative costs, but certainly not three months' interest worth of costs (which is what they usually want to charge). Should you object? Yes. After all, if rates were higher you'd have to pay an IRD; since rates are lower, you shouldn't have to. If they insist you pay a penalty, then you should point out what a good customer you are and how many different products you hold with them: RRSPs, chequing and savings accounts, GICs, mutual funds, loans — everything. If they still insist, you may have to pay the IRD since it's in the terms and conditions of your mortgage. However, you may want to start looking for a mortgagor who places a higher value on your business. And the next time you sign a mortgage document, try to get them to take out the paragraph about an interest penalty when rates are lower.

Compounding Interest

The rate at which interest is charged on the interest owing on your mortgage will affect the total amount of interest you pay. The more frequent the compounding, the more interest paid. Financial institutions can use any frequency they wish for compounding the interest. Most conventional mortgages have interest compounded half-yearly, not in advance. However, some variable-rate mortgages compound interest monthly. Ask the financial institution what the equivalent rate would be if the interest were compounded yearly or half-yearly, not in advance. For example, a variable-rate mortgage with a stated, or "nominal," rate of 10 percent has an equivalent, or "effective," rate of 10 percent when compounded annually, 10.25 percent when compounded half-yearly and 10.47 percent when compounded monthly. So, the more often the interest is calculated, the more interest you'll pay on the mortgage.

What Exactly Does "Not in Advance" Mean?

When you pay for something before you actually have use of it, you're paying "in advance." The most common in-advance payment is rent. For example, a rent payment on June 1 gives you the right to use the apartment for the month of June.

When you pay for something *after* you've used it, you're paying for it "not in advance." If, for example, you stay in a hotel, you don't actually pay for the hotel room until you've finished using it. That's "not in advance." The same principal applies to your mortgage payment. When you make your June mortgage payment, you're paying for May. When you make your July payment, you're paying for June, and so on. You're always paying for the use of the money after you've had use of it.

What Is the Interest Adjustment Date?

The interest adjustment date, or IAD, is the date on which the mortgage term will begin. This date is usually the first day of the month following the closing. So, if you close on September 14, your mortgage term will actually begin on October 1. However, since you've had the use of the financial institution's money since September 14, you will be charged interest on that money back to September 14. This accrued interest is usually due with your first regular monthly mortgage payment.

You should try to make your closing date as close to the end of a month as you can so that the accrued interest will be as low as possible. You can calculate the accrued interest you will owe using the following formula:

$$\frac{\text{Total mortgage amount x Interest rate}}{365} \quad \text{x} \quad \begin{array}{l}\text{no. of days until} \\ \text{the beginning of} \\ \text{the month}\end{array} \quad = \quad \begin{array}{l}\text{Accrued} \\ \text{interest} \\ \text{payable}\end{array}$$

Bobby McFarlain is closing his new home on May 18. He is taking out a $74,000 mortgage at 9.5 percent. The IAD will be June 1 because that's the first day of the month following the closing. The accrued interest Bobby will have to pay, along with his first mortgage payment (on July 1, since the payment is made "not in advance"), is:

$$\frac{\$74,000 \times 9.5\%}{365} \quad \text{x} \quad 14 \quad = \quad \$269.64$$

Property Taxes

Some people find it difficult to deal with lump-sum property tax bills. To provide a convenient, worry-free way of budgeting for annual taxes, most financial institutions will arrange with local tax authorities for realty tax bills to be forwarded to them for payment on your behalf. This means you can spread the tax payment over a period of time rather than facing large bills all at once.

An amount is added to your regular mortgage payment to cover the taxes. To ensure that when taxes are due there will be sufficient funds in your tax account to cover the billing in full, a tax holdback may be required. This is an amount held back from the proceeds of the mortgage loan.

> Paula and Gerry Wilsome have just purchased a new home. Their property taxes are due in January, March, June and September each year. Their annual taxes are $1,600 and they are making monthly mortgage payments. Therefore, $133.33 is added to their mortgage payment each month.
>
> The Wilsomes will make their first mortgage payment on August 1. So in September, when the third quarterly payment is due, they will have paid a total of $266.66 into their tax account. Since this is less ($133.34 less) than the amount payable in September, a tax holdback of $133.34 is made to cover the difference.

This holdback can put you in a bit of a cash crunch. After all, if you get less of an advance, you'll have to make up the difference from your own pocket. You might as well be making your own tax payments. Most financial institutions will waive tax holdbacks if you indicate that you are aware of the potential tax shortage and are prepared to cover it when the taxes become due and payable.

You may also want to consider paying your own property tax. After all, while the extra amount goes into a tax account, you may not be paid as high an interest rate on that account as you would be in a regular savings account. You should offer to provide proof of tax payment each time your taxes are paid so the financial institution doesn't have to worry about losing their "first place" standing. You see, if you don't pay your property taxes, under provincial law those unpaid taxes are a lien against the property and bump the first mortgagor into second place behind the government.

Mortgage Renewals

Your term is up and now it's time to renew your mortgage. There are a number of points you should consider:

- If you think you may need additional funds during the year, you may wish to refinance your mortgage at renewal. Maybe you plan to do some travelling. Perhaps you want to redo the kitchen. Or maybe you've run up some debt you need to pay off. Since a mortgage is the least costly form of financing available, by refinancing at renewal, you can get the extra money you need at the lowest possible cost.

- Renewal time is the perfect opportunity to pay down your mortgage. Since a mortgage is completely open at the time of renewal, you can make a payment against your principal of whatever amount you choose. Even a small amount can have a significant impact in terms of interest saved over the life of the mortgage.

- If your payments are lower either because interest rates have fallen or because there have been significant decreases in your principal, you may wish to consider maintaining the same payment amount. By maintaining the same mortgage payment amount, you will be paying more of your principal, reducing your amortization and saving in interest over the life of the mortgage.

- If you aren't already contributing to your RRSP, then do so, starting now. If your payments are lower, you could contribute the difference to an RRSP. Since you successfully worked the higher mortgage payment into your budget, contributing the difference to an RRSP shouldn't be a hardship.

Early Renewal

Many financial institutions allow you to renegotiate your mortgage at any time in advance of the mortgage's maturing, provided the mortgage is in good standing. The new mortgage can be for any term. If current rates are lower than the rate on the existing mortgage, some financial institutions will blend both rates for the remaining term. For example, if you have a mortgage at 12 percent with a one-year term remaining, and you renew now at nine percent for five years, the interest you pay will be a blend of the 12 and the nine percent rates. In effect, you pay 12 percent for the remaining one-year term, and nine percent thereafter. However, the benefit is that if you think interest rates are as low as they are going to go, you get to lock in that low rate now. You don't have to wait a year, when you might see the rates go up.

Some financial institutions will let you renew early, but charge you a LIC or IRD, calculated on the difference between the interest paid on the existing mortgage and the interest rate currently charged for the equivalent remaining term.

> Melville Drake has six months remaining on his three-year mortgage. He has decided to renew early. His existing mortgage is at 12.5 percent and he wants to renew for five years at 9.5 percent. The interest penalty charged would be calculated based on the difference between his existing interest rate (12.5 percent) and the rate for the equivalent remaining term (six months at 9.5 percent).

The benefits and costs of early renewal vary from person to person. Some people may save money, and others may pay more than necessary. If you are thinking about renewing early, consider the following:

- where you think interest rates are headed
- the cost of the loss of interest penalty (if applicable)
- whether you have the immediate cash to pay the loss of interest penalty
- the amount of time remaining on your current term
- which new term to choose

If you are considering early renewal, you have two decisions to make:

- whether or not to early renew based on where interest rates are going, and

- how to finance that early renewal.

If rates are going higher, and the mortgage is near maturity, you can renew early and lock in the interest rate for as long a period of time as you wish. If, however, you still have a significant term remaining on your mortgage, you must weigh the cost of the loss of interest penalty against the potential savings in interest over the long term. This can be a difficult decision to make since the variables involved (i.e., the interest rate at renewal of the original term and at renewal of the new term) cannot be predicted. If you believe that interest rates will be higher at your existing renewal date, you can renew early to protect yourself from that higher rate. However, if you believe that rates will decline further, you should not renew early since you will be locking yourself into a higher rate than necessary. If you believe rates will remain stable, there is no benefit to renewing early.

If a lost interest penalty is charged, you can usually finance this in one of two ways:

- you can pay the lost interest penalty up front, or

- you can capitalize the lost interest penalty (i.e., add the penalty to your principal). However, if you choose to capitalize the lost interest penalty, you should know that you will, in fact, be paying interest on the interest. Since the lost interest penalty is being added to the principal, over the remaining amortization, you will pay a significant amount of interest on that (lost) interest (penalty).

When you are ready to move, unless your term is up you may have to pay a lost interest penalty in order to discharge the mortgage early. Of course, if current rates are higher than your existing mortgage rate, you shouldn't have to pay anything since your financial institution can lend that money at a higher rate. Some may want to charge you an administration fee of some type (or an IRD based on a minimum of three months), but I'd kick and scream.

If, in fact, interest rates are lower than the interest rate on your current mortgage, you may have to pay an IRD. However, most financial institutions offer you two alternatives to avoid this:

• you can "port" the mortgage to your new house, or

• you can have the buyer of your old house assume the existing mortgage.

Porting

If you want to take your mortgage with you when you move, you can use the portability option most institutions offer. By porting the mortgage, you can continue taking advantage of lower interest rates, or you can blend the existing mortgage with a new one if additional financing is required. This may eliminate the need for a much costlier second mortgage. It also eliminates the interest penalties that apply to a straight early discharge of an existing mortgage.This option is especially advantageous when the interest rate on the existing mortgage is lower than currently available for a new mortgage.

Since a new mortgage document must be drawn up and registered on title, normal appraisal and legal fees are payable. A nominal portability fee may also apply.

Assuming

If you are moving and don't want to take your mortgage with you, an assumable feature will allow the buyers of your home to take over the mortgage, providing they meet normal lending criteria. In fact, if your mortgage interest rate is lower than those currently available, this can be an added feature that may help you sell your home even faster.

❈ ❈

Just because someone assumes your mortgage does not mean you are necessarily off the hook for the liability. You must get a release from your mortgage company to ensure you are no longer liable for the debt. Some mortgage companies automatically offer a release. With others, you have to make the request. *Whatever it takes, if your mortgage is being assumed, make sure you get a release.*

❈ ❈

Buying Down the Interest Rate

If you are trying to sell your house and you want to make your existing mortgage very attractive to buyers, you can arrange with the lender to prepay a portion of the interest. Called a "buy down," it allows the person buying your house to assume a mortgage at an interest rate lower than the current stated rate. You can then add the amount of interest you're planning to prepay onto the purchase price of your property. As everyone knows, an offer of a low mortgage, particularly when current rates are high, can be extremely attractive to a buyer. For example, if current mortgage rates are at 12 percent and you buy down the rate to 10 percent, you may generate a lot of interest in your "home for sale."

Vendor Take Back

Sometimes as an incentive to buyers, sellers offer to finance the mortgage themselves, usually at a rate lower than those offered by financial institutions. A "vendor take back" mortgage exists when the seller provides some or all of the financing in order to sell the property. Financial institutions are not involved in this transaction. The borrower then makes payments to the vendor, not to a financial institution.

Switching

If you're unhappy with your mortgagor, shop around. If you decide to move and don't want to incur all the costs associated with obtaining a new mortgage, check to see if the new financial institution offers a "switching" or "transfer-in" program. Many do as a way of winning business. When a mortgage is transferred, rather than discharged by the original lender, it is assigned by the original lender to the new lender. You usually do not have to pay appraisal, legal or transfer-in fees. However, there may be a charge by the existing lender. Because of this, most people choose to switch when they have an open mortgage or when a closed mortgage comes up for renewal. In order to qualify for a transfer, both you and your mortgage must meet the new financial institution's lending criteria.

Discharges

You've paid the whole thing off. Now you want to remove the mortgage charge from your home, called "discharging" the mortgage. It's easy. You (or your lawyer) request a discharge and your financial institution issues a discharge statement that you (or your lawyer) register on title.

Insurance and Your Mortgage

Since your home is likely to be your single largest investment, you may want to protect that investment. Many financial institutions offer mortgage life insurance at an affordable and competitive price. The eligibility requirements are usually quite simple to meet. Before buying mortgage life insurance from your mortgagor, however, shop around. Term insurance may, in fact, be a cheaper way of financing protection on your home. Here are the facts you should consider:

• Term rates will increase, usually every five years, while your mortgage life insurance rate will typically remain the same over the life of the mortgage. Sometimes the mortgage life insurance rates will go up if the group rate for the entire plan increases.

- Mortgage life insurance is not calculated on the declining balance of your mortgage. So even if you've paid off half your mortgage, your mortgage life insurance premium is still based on the original mortgage amount.

- For most mortgage life insurance plans, there is a maximum amount of insurance you can get. If your total mortgages exceed this maximum, the difference isn't covered under the plan.

- Mortgage life insurance offers joint coverage from about 40 percent more than single coverage (usually based on the age of the older applicant). To achieve the same level of joint coverage on both you and your spouse with term insurance, you'd have to pay two sets of premiums (i.e., there's no discount).

The best thing to do in making a decision about how to insure your mortgage is to have an insurance agent work out the figures for term insurance (including the likely increases in premiums every five years) based on your age, sex and health, your need for single or joint coverage and the amount of insurance you want for a specific period of time (and estimate of the amount of time it'll take to retire your mortgage). Remember to have the agent factor in the declining balance when figuring out the term insurance figure. Then compare that figure with the rates being offered by financial institutions for their mortgage life insurance over the same length of time. Do the math. It's worth it.

Some financial institutions now offer income-interruption and/or disability insurance for mortgagees. In essence, if you are laid off (you must be involuntarily unemployed) or become disabled, the insurance will either make your full monthly payment or pay the interest so that you don't fall behind. As with mortgage life insurance, you should weigh the cost of this insurance against the cost of being covered under a plan you buy personally.

THE MORTGAGE CHECKLIST

When shopping for a mortgage, use this checklist to compare options and make your decision. You should check three or four financial institutions before you make your final decision unless there are specific features offered by only one or two that you just have to have.

☐ What are the current interest rates for:
    6-month open
    6-month closed
    Open (1 year or more)
    Closed
        1 year
        2 year
        3 year
        4 year
        5 year
        Other
    Variable-rate

☐ What amortization periods are available?
    Can the amortization be shortened or lengthened at renewal?

☐ Is the mortgage convertible?
    Is there a minimum term?
    How much notice do you have to give, if any?

☐ How is the interest rate calculated?
    Semi-annually, not in advance
    Other

☐ Are there prepayment options?
    Is there a maximum that can be prepaid?
    Is there a minimum that must be prepaid?
    When can the prepayment be made?
    How often can you prepay?
    Can payment amounts be increased?
    By how much?

☐ Can you renew early?
    Is there an interest penalty?
    Under what circumstances?
    Can you renew early with a blended rate?

☐ What payment frequencies are available?
Are faster-pay frequencies available?

☐ Is pre-approval available?
Is there a rate guarantee?
For how long?

☐ Is the mortgage assumable?

☐ Is the mortgage portable?
What portability features are included (straight port, port and increase, port and decrease)?
Will port and increase mortgages be blended?
What are the minimum terms, if any?

☐ Can you pay your own property taxes?
If not, does there have to be a tax holdback?
What rate of interest is paid on tax accounts?
How can you get higher interest (i.e., comparable with a savings rate)?
What interest rate is charged if the tax account goes into a debit position?

☐ Costs for:
     prepayment IRD
     prepayment administration fee
     renewal
     early renewal
     assumability
     portability
     mortgage set-up
     appraisal
     discharge
     changing payment frequency

☐ Is mortgage life insurance available?
Is income interruption/disability insurance available?

69

4 What Lenders Look For

Every lending transaction has two sets of expectations. You expect lenders to do everything possible to ensure you get the loan and, most often, they will. On the other hand, lenders expect you to pay back the loan under the terms agreed. If you miss or delay payments, you demonstrate a lack of commitment to meeting your side of the bargain. That's one reason previous histories of missed payments are very carefully considered.

Once you have completed the loan interview, the lender does a credit investigation to confirm the statements you have made. It's not that they don't trust you. They simply want to make sure that their decisions are based on accurate, comprehensive information. That means verifying your identification and financial details and developing a perspective of your past financial performance. Lenders always complete the credit verification before proceeding with their decisions. Don't assume that because you have been dealing with a financial institution for a long time, or because they have lent to you before without incident, that you'll automatically get the loan. Each time you apply to borrow money, you are carefully scrutinized to see if you will qualify.

Credit investigations are done by calling upon a number of resources:

- internal records, for existing customers
- other financial institutions' records
- credit bureau reports
- other creditors' records
- employment records

The primary requirements used to establish your credit worthiness are usually described as either the Three C's or the Five C's of credit. I like the Five C's because it breaks down what lenders look for into five distinct areas.

The Five C's of Credit

All of the following elements are very carefully considered before the lender makes a final decision:

- Character
- Capacity
- Credit
- Capital
- Collateral

Let's take a look at each of these in detail.

Character

This refers to your intention to repay the loan and is very carefully considered, because few people change their character after credit has been extended. Lenders learn a lot about your character during the loan interview. If you are open and honest, providing all the information lenders need to make their decisions, it not only makes their job easier, it builds confidence in your integrity. In fact, if you are completely honest but do not immediately qualify for the loan, lenders may take the time to counsel you on ways to get the loan.

As they do their credit investigation, lenders may hear other character-related comments. They will check your references to see what other creditors have to say about you. Most lenders have the common sense to know that they have to weigh these statements carefully. They look for corroboration before giving the comments full validity.

If you qualify in all areas of the investigation but your intent to repay seems dubious, you may represent a high level of risk. Here are some things lenders look at in evaluating character:

- **Your Level of Debt Involvement**
  Is your debt load reasonable for your current level of income, or are you overextended? If you have taken on debt that is controllable now but would present a problem should a small financial setback occur, lenders will weigh this carefully. For example, if you have a mortgage that is due for renewal and rates have increased dramatically, you could be in a much more difficult position with a high debt load. The likelihood is that the mortgage payment will be made before the loan payment. Knowing this, lenders may decide not to approve your loan.

- **Your Employment Record**
  Job stability is important for analysing character. Many job changes over the past few years may be positive or negative. If you are talented and aggressively seeking increases in income, it can be very positive. However, if you have not been able to maintain job continuity, switching for little or no financial or professional improvement, this may indicate instability. If you have made several employment changes recently (and over your career), you should be prepared with good explanations for why you moved around. If your reasons are weak, this will work against you.

  An unstable job history may indicate an inability to maintain regular payments. If you became unemployed, lenders know the natural reaction is to cover your living expenses first: food, rent, immediate expenses. The loan payment may become less of a priority. Your intentions to repay may have appeared to be good, but a change in your circumstances may alter your priorities.

- **Residence Stability**

  A major portion of your personal income is spent maintaining your residence. Each time you move, you incur costs and the amount spent on maintaining a residence may change. A lack of stability in residence (renting less than one year or moving often) may also indicate a lack of commitment to a regular routine. That can translate into a lack of commitment to routine payments. Lenders also have to consider how hard it would be to find you if your loan defaulted and you had moved.

  Since home ownership is a major commitment, an established mortgage payment made over more than one year will give lenders a good indication of your ability and willingness to make regular payments. The same is true if you rent and have maintained the same residence for two years and more.

- **Purpose of the Loan**

  What you want to do with the loan is a good indicator of character. The reason for the loan may reflect your attitude to the necessities of life. Most people borrow for good reasons such as buying a car or renovating their homes. Generally, large purchases require planning in terms of associated expenses. Sometimes, however, lenders receive requests from people who have not included all the appropriate facts in their purchasing decisions.

  Before you decide how much you need, make sure you've considered all the facts. For example, if you're asking for a $20,000 loan to renovate your home, have you considered what would happen if the renovation were more expensive than you originally anticipated? Likewise, if you already have a high debt load and want a loan to buy a new toy, such as a boat or motorcycle, lenders will look carefully at your priorities in spending money.

The area of character lenders examine most closely is your stability. Employment, residence and past credit repayment consistency all reflect what you will likely do in the future. The lender's judgment of your character during the interview will be based on:

- whether you have been honest in presenting your financial situation

- his or her impression of you in terms of your attitude, manner or responses

- your consistency in providing the information they need to complete the application

When they do the investigation, lenders will uncover other items they can use to make a judgment in terms of your character. They will be looking for things such as:

- your demonstrated responsibility in handling your finances as indicated by careful planning and management (e.g., you have no legal judgments or proceedings against you)

- whether you have insurance (indicating that you are planning for the future)

- whether you show evidence of financial planning (indicating that you are structuring your financial affairs carefully in view of income and the quality of your assets)

- your stability (e.g., length and consistency of employment, residence and the number of times relocated, and consistent career growth)

- your value system in terms of prioritizing your expenditures (e.g., little impulse spending, a balance of assets and liabilities)

- your expectations in terms of both the purpose of the loan and the building of assets in relationship to your income

Very few loans are declined merely on character assessment alone. However, character assessment does support other, more credit-specific information, such as capacity and credit history. Collateral and capital also reflect on your character. If you have established assets over the years, you have also usually established good credit character.

Capacity

Capacity refers to your ability to repay the loan. Without the capacity to repay the financial commitment, there is little point in a lender giving you the money. Here are some of the factors on which a capacity judgment is often made:

- **Income Level**
  This is the most important aspect in determining your capacity because it indicates the amount of discretionary income you have. Lenders may look at the amount of investing you are doing and the amount of money being spent on vacations, clothing or entertainment. Part of being able to demonstrate a good capacity involves creating assets. If you find you are living on a shoestring, using a budget may help you get your finances under control.

- **Repayment Terms**
  The repayment terms are also a major consideration. The repayment level must have some relationship to your discretionary income so that the monthly payment will not be made at the expense of other necessities. When that happens, lenders know you are much more likely to make late payments or default on the loan.

  By allowing longer repayment terms, the total monthly amount can be reduced to fit in with your cash flow. However, there is

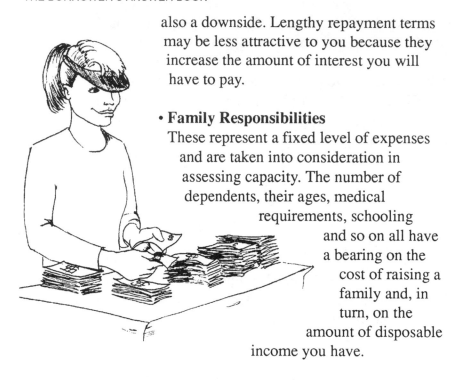

also a downside. Lengthy repayment terms may be less attractive to you because they increase the amount of interest you will have to pay.

- **Family Responsibilities**

These represent a fixed level of expenses and are taken into consideration in assessing capacity. The number of dependents, their ages, medical requirements, schooling and so on all have a bearing on the cost of raising a family and, in turn, on the amount of disposable income you have.

- **Job Stability**

This factor helps lenders determine how stable your income will be. Since previous and existing work habits extend into the future, you must have demonstrated a reasonable measure of stability over at least the past two years.

If you are a young borrower with little previous employment history, lenders will look at your family background, educational qualifications and other general characteristics.

When lenders look at your capacity, they are trying to predict your ability to repay based on current information and future events. Since the repayment is a thing of the future, lenders have to consider your capacity to repay in the future.

Calculating TDS

One way of determining your capacity to repay is by calculating your total debt service (TDS) ratio. Your TDS looks at how much you make, how much debt you currently have and how much of a strain on your cash flow the new loan payment will be. Financial institutions have a limit on how high your TDS can go, and if you're over that limit, they won't give you the money. This is in both their interest and yours. From a lender's perspective, they have to worry that if your circumstances change, you won't be able to service your debt (i.e., make your payments on time.) From your perspective, too high a TDS can put severe stress on you.

By the end of the interview, the lender will have calculated your TDS and determined whether you immediately qualify in terms of capacity. If you don't, that does not mean they will not lend to you. It simply means a more creative approach will have to be taken. For example, if you wanted a one-year loan but your TDS ratio is higher than acceptable, by extending the term of the loan your payment amount will go down and you may be able to bring the TDS into line.

TDS is calculated using the following formula:

$$\frac{\text{Total monthly payments} \times 100}{\text{Gross income}} = \text{Total debt service ratio } \%$$

For example:

Monthly Payments:

Rent	$700.00
Car Loan	350.00
Credit Card Payments	100.00
New Loan Payment	325.00
Total	$1,475.00

Monthly Income: $3,900.00

TDS calculation:

$$\frac{1,475 \times 100}{3,900} = 37.8\%$$

When you're thinking about applying for a loan, it would be well worth your while to calculate your TDS to determine if you will qualify. If you come out around 30 percent or less, you're probably okay. If you're significantly higher, you may have to do some creative thinking to figure a way to get your TDS down.

One way is to take the loan for a longer term (or choose a longer amortization on a mortgage). Another way is simply to borrow less. You do have options, and an experienced, professional lender will help you to see them.

In determining your capacity to handle a mortgage payment, lenders look at both your TDS and your gross debt service (GDS) ratio. Your GDS consists of the total of the principal and interest, plus the property taxes and heating costs. Typically, this total should not exceed 35 percent of your total gross income (i.e., your income before taxes). In calculating your TDS for a mortgage, all of the items in the GDS calculation are included, as well as any payments you may be making on debts such as credit cards, car loans and the like. Your TDS shouldn't exceed 40 percent of your gross annual income.

Credit

Your credit history provides a snapshot of how you have handled debt in the past and, by extension, how you may handle debt in the future. If you are an existing customer of the financial institution to which you are applying for the loan, they will check out the activity on your accounts (e.g., overdraft management, NSF cheques written, previous loan repayment history) when analysing your credit history.

The other way lenders check up on you is by using the credit bureau. The credit bureau provides credit references that cover the credit history of most people. Lenders will also call existing creditors, your mortgage holder or your landlord for further references.

The credit bureau report contains identifying information that lenders use to confirm your identity. Your current address and employer are listed, as well as the number of addresses and employers since the file was opened. This gives lenders a pretty good handle on your stability. Any information of public record such a bankruptcies, writs and judgments are noted, along with a detailed list of transactions, which outlines your paying habits.

Checking Your Credit History

You are entitled to check your credit history, though sometimes you have to pay a fee to do so. If you're not sure of your credit standing, or if you experience significant changes such as a divorce, check your credit history.

You may not realize that when you're married, often your credit file will be cross-referenced with that of your spouse. If you separate, the files may remain cross-referenced. And if you've ever applied for credit jointly, your file may remain a joint file unless you specifically request it be changed. This is particularly significant if one of you has a more trouble-free payment history than the other. The best way to deal with this is to try to maintain separate credit identities.

Often, when women are divorced or widowed, they are surprised to learn that as far as the financial world is concerned, they do not exist. Unfortunately, many women rely on their husbands' credit identities. They have no credit identity of their own.

As a woman in today's highly complex world, you owe yourself a credit identity. Start small, maybe with a charge card. Take a small loan and pay it back as quickly as you can. Build a credit history for yourself and create your credit identity. It may stand you in very good stead should you ever need to borrow money.

If you plan to apply for a loan or have recently been turned down, this would be a good reason to check your credit history. Credit bureaus are not infallible. In fact, lots of people have had the unhappy experience of finding information on their credit bureau reports that is incorrect. Mistakes happen. But if you don't identify them, you can't correct them.

Freddy Graham was applying for a substantial mortgage. Everything looked fine until the lender called Freddy to say he had an R9 (not good!) on his credit bureau report. The lender thought Freddy should do some checking into this since it was for a small amount – only $100 – from a financial institution. In fact, the lender told Freddy, "I bet it's a renewal fee for a credit card."

Since Freddy had never dealt with the financial institution that had recorded the R9, he was really at a loss about what it could be for. Then he remembered. About two years earlier, he had been sent an unsolicited credit card. He didn't want the card, so he simply trashed it. Mistake! They had charged the annual fee to the card and had reported the nonpayment to the credit bureau.

Now Freddy was mad! How dare they! He called the financial institution, explained the situation and insisted that the credit bureau be informed of the error. He also insisted on receiving a printout of the credit bureau report so he could ensure the R9 had been removed. It took several follow-up calls and a lot of persistence, but the R9 was finally removed.

The first step in clarifying any mistakes on your credit history file is to find out where your file is. Look in the telephone directory for the credit bureau closest to you. If there isn't one, ask your bank or any company with whom you have a credit card for the name of whom to contact.

The next step is to call or write and ask for an appointment to review your credit history. Someone at the credit bureau will go through your file with you.

If you spot mistakes, you will be asked to provide written proof before your file can be changed. If you cannot supply written proof, give the facts to the credit bureau. They will check into them and when they're confirmed, your file will be updated. If the facts cannot be confirmed, the offending information may be removed or noted as "in dispute," depending on where you live. Different provinces have different legislation regarding how disputes are handled.

Once information on your credit history has been corrected, the credit bureau must notify members who have made inquiries about you in the previous months (as required by provincial legislation).

Generally, credit bureaus are not allowed to keep information older than seven years on file. However, this, too, depends on provincial legislation.

If you approach getting credit as a shopping expedition, you have to be careful about how often a credit bureau inquiry is done for you. A listing of all credit bureau inquiries is provided on the credit bureau report. Many recent inquiries could indicate to a lender that you have been approaching other institutions and are "credit seeking." This is a warning signal for lenders since it often indicates you've either been turned down elsewhere or have a higher level of debt than you may be able to manage.

That doesn't mean you shouldn't shop around. What it does mean is that you have to be careful how far you go when you are shopping. You don't need the aggravation of having three or four credit bureau inquiries showing up on your sparkling record.

When you're shopping, you have to decide what you're shopping for:

- the best service
- the lowest rate
- the most attractive loan features

Most of your shopping can be done before you actually apply for the loan.

Not all credit grantors are members of the credit bureau. Some records are not up to date because some companies report their experiences with customers at irregular intervals. For this reason, some past or current accounts may not be on file with the bureau. Unfortunately, unless you have access to the credit bureau, there's no way of knowing what will show up. Your best bet is to be open and up front. Your honesty will be appreciated.

Access to credit bureau reports are controlled by legislation, and you must be informed before a credit bureau report may be requested. By signing the loan application, you authorized the obtaining of a credit bureau report. There are four ways lenders obtain credit bureau reports:

- They can get a verbal report over the phone.

- They can receive a written report from the bureau.

- If they have a credit bureau terminal, they can access a written copy at their location.

- Some financial institutions' credit systems interface with the credit bureau. These systems automatically do a credit bureau check and provide lenders with the information gathered.

Your reputation and credit rating must be good, as must your ability to meet past obligations. If you have established credit at stores, other financial institutions, etc., and have demonstrated an ability to meet your obligations on time, lenders have no reason to think your performance at their company will be any different.

Of course, your past record has to be considered in light of your income and position at the time of borrowing. For example, if 10 years ago you were late with a number of payments on a car loan, but since that time you have demonstrated a commitment to meet your obligations, this past performance should be seen as a whole. Lenders should not use single episodes to support a negative decision. If you find one who does, shop around.

If you have not previously used credit and have no credit history, lenders will look very carefully at your occupation, earnings and assets. This is often of particular issue with young borrowers and women who have not established their own credit ratings. Often I hear complaints such as, "Financial institutions won't lend to me unless I can prove I don't need the money." While this sometimes seems to be the way things work (particularly when financial institutions are being very conservative in their lending), if you don't have a credit history, you make it very hard for a lender to get a good picture of your commitment to repay.

If you've had past delinquencies or defaults, lenders look more closely at your situation. They don't want to be in the position of constantly having to call you for collection purposes. They know that each time they do, they run the risk of alienating you. As well, collection activities are expensive in terms of the time spent, resources needed and the chance of default. If you know there is something negative that may show up on your credit bureau report, you should tell the lender about it during your interview, and explain the circumstances then.

Capital

Capital, or net worth, is the assessment of your total financial assets and financial security. Net worth is based on the total value of your assets (real estate, investment portfolio, RRSPs and other equity such as automobiles) less your liabilities (loans, mortgages). Because personal and household goods are not as marketable, they are not usually used in calculating net worth.

Net worth must be considered in relation to your age. Mature people with long credit histories may reasonably be expected to have accumulated far greater net worth than a young person just beginning a new career. Let's take a look at how net worth is calculated and evaluated.

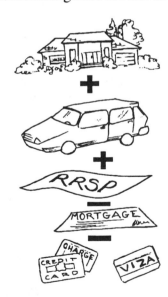

	ASSETS	LIABILITIES
Market value of home	$175,000	
Mortgage		$125,000
Account balances	2,800	
Loans		18,000
Investment portfolio	22,000	
Credit card balances		4,800
RRSPs	32,000	
1992 Toyota	22,000	
Totals	$253,800	$147,800
Total assets	$253,800	
less total liabilities	-$147,800	
Net Worth	$106,000	

In looking at your capital, or net worth, lenders are trying to determine how you have spent your money in the past. Here are some of the things they look for:

1. The proportion of debt to assets:

- Are assets heavily financed?

- What would happen if your financial circumstances changed negatively?

2. The quality of the assets acquired, which reflects your choices and priorities:

- Are the values recorded realistic?

- Will these assets retain their value?

- Can the assets be easily liquidated?

3. The type of debt you've acquired and your ability to structure debt:

- Are your long-term assets being financed by appropriate debt?

- Are you acquiring debt for little return in terms of long-term benefit?

- What does this say about your cash flow management?

Capital acts as both an extension of character and a source for collateral. It indicates your ability to manage your personal finances. If after 10 or 15 years you've established little net worth, this could indicate you have not been able to save.

Lenders know that some people make major purchases that are financed because they find it easier to work those payments into their cash flow than to save. These people may not have accumulated a high level of net worth, but they may have a consistent credit history of loan repayment. Lenders know these can be wonderful customers to cultivate.

Collateral

There are a number of loan situations for which lenders will want to look at your ownership of assets to secure the loan with collateral. For example, if you wish to secure a loan that is very large in relation to your net worth (i.e., people with other debts, first-time borrowers, or self-employed and commissioned sales people), you may have to provide collateral as security for the loan. Sometimes people choose to use collateral to reduce the rate of interest they pay on the loan.

The assets taken as collateral serve as security for the financial institution. If you default on the loan, the assets can be liquidated to provide all or at least partial payment of the loan. Collateral also helps to ensure you have a vested interest in repaying the loan. When collateral is taken, the financial institution exercises control over the asset, preventing you from disposing of it and redirecting the funds elsewhere.

Various types of assets can be used as security. However, some assets can be accepted only at part of their face value, such as stock certificates (see page 26).

In qualifying collateral, (i.e., determining its usability and appropriateness as security) financial institutions use the following criteria:

- the asset must be readily identifiable

- the asset must have a relatively stable value and not be highly speculative in nature

- the asset must be realistically valued based on current market value

- the asset must be readily salable, in terms of both the condition of the collateral and in terms of an established market

- the asset must be assignable and transferrable (e.g., RRSP assets are not assignable as collateral)

Self-Employed Customers

People who are self-employed present special circumstances. Lenders usually conduct a credit bureau check on both the person and the business. They will also want to look at your current and previous year's income tax returns and financial statements (personal and business). And they will likely use the Registry Office to clarify the ownership of your assets and check with the Better Business Bureau to uncover additional information about the business.

Typical Situations

Here are some of the typical situations of would-be borrowers, and the areas lenders will look at closely for each. If you can

provide satisfactory answers to these questions, you are much
more likely to get the loan.

Young, first-time borrowers:
- Do you have a credit history?
- What indicates job and income stability?
- Do you have assets to provide collateral?
- Is a guarantor available?

Self-employed borrowers:
- Have you demonstrated stability of income?
- What is your current debt load?
- Can the lender check your work habits and responsibility?
- Can lender differentiate between your personal and
  business finances?

Consolidation of debts:
- Have you consolidated before?
- Does this indicate a lack of financial control?
- What precipitated this situation?

Funds needed for home improvement:
- Do you own your own home?
- How large is your mortgage?

Funds needed for RRSP contribution:
- Do you normally deal with the financial institution to
  which you're applying for the loan?
- If not, why have you chosen this financial institution for
  the money? If you've been declined elsewhere, this may
  become apparent during the credit investigation. Be up
  front with the lender.

Funds needed for pleasure purposes:
- Do you have the ability for repayment?
- Are you committed to repayment?
- What would happen if your financial circumstances
  changed?

Seasonal employees or retirees:
- Are your other debt obligations fulfilled?
- Do you have the ability (i.e., the capacity) to repay the loan?
- Is your income sufficiently stable?

Several employers:
- Do you have the ability to repay the loan?
- Do you have alternative payment sources if you were to become unemployed?
- Are you of good character and do you take your current employment seriously (i.e., you won't be fired or resigned)?

Not known to the lender or other branch personnel:
- Do you live or work near the branch to which you're applying? If not, the lender will want to know why you chose his or her branch. Are you shopping? Have you been declined elsewhere?

Divorced and receiving alimony/support:
- Could you meet the debt obligation if the alimony payments were interrupted or stopped?

Divorced and paying alimony/support:
- Is there an increase in alimony/support built into your separation/divorce agreement?
- How would this affect your future cash flow?

Inactivity in work record with gaps:
- What did you do between jobs?
- How have you met debt obligations in the past?

You want money to cover "current expenses":
- What are these current expenses?
- Are you overextended financially?
- What is your credit history?

Constantly borrowing money:
- Are you acquiring assets?
- Are you having trouble budgeting and managing cash flow?
- Do you have any overlapping loans?
- If you became unemployed, how would that affect your ability to meet your financial commitments?

Managing Your Credit History Is Your Responsibility

No one has more control over your credit history than you. When you're granted credit, be very careful how you use it. Never let incorrect reporting to a credit bureau go uncorrected, no matter how much effort it takes. And recognize that even small slips, such as late payments and NSF cheques, can have a long-term negative impact on your credit history. Having access to credit can be extremely important. Misuse of credit can make your life miserable. Don't charge items you aren't completely sure you'll be able to pay for. Never be late with a payment. And never write cheques unless you know you have sufficient funds to cover them. The interest costs aren't the only costs you'll have to contend with. Lost credibility is a lot harder to recover.

5 The Loan Interview

Now it's time to ask for the loan. If you've never done this before, you may be nervous. That's natural. After all, you're going to be telling the lender a lot of personal information about yourself. And you may feel embarrassed by your financial circumstances if you've got yourself into a bit of a tight spot. The fact is, borrowing money has become a way of life for most of us. People borrow for all sorts of reasons. Whether you are building your assets or rectifying your financial situation, credit can be an important tool. Sometimes, the best of us let our finances get out of hand. It's okay. After all, as a friend of mine is apt to remind me, "It's not where you start off, it's where you end up that counts."

The data the lender will use to make the credit assessment comes from the information you provide during the loan interview. If you've borrowed before, this all happens quickly since the lender will likely have a record of your last loan and will simply need to update the information. For new borrowers, or those borrowing from a different lender, the process takes a little longer.

The main reasons lenders conduct a loan interview is to:

• establish positive identification to prevent fraud

• gather reliable and complete information about you

• provide you with what you need to know and help you
  determine the credit option(s) that best meets your needs.

The data lenders gather during the interview helps them to ensure they are making sound decisions. If they haven't been able to learn all they need to know, they may have to contact you again for additional information, which delays the loan approval, or they may simply decline the loan. Your objective in going through the process is to give the lender all the information needed so a decision can be reached.

Preparing for the Interview

The better prepared you are for your loan interview, the more likely you are to get the loan. If you're a first-time borrower or borrowing from a different financial institution, start by developing a relationship with the financial institution from which you'll be borrowing. Lenders are often more willing to provide financing if you are already a customer. So, the first step is to open an account with the institution from whom you'll be seeking financing.

The more business you have with a financial institution, the more likely they will be to lend to you. Lenders hate putting their relationships with good customers at risk. However, that doesn't mean you have to have all your business with one financial institution right off the bat. The fact is, if you can offer the lender other business (as well as the loan business) when you are negotiating the terms of the loan, you may be able to negotiate a better interest rate. But a strong showing at the financial institution where you're borrowing will likely work to your advantage.

In preparing for the loan interview, there are a number of questions for which you should be prepared. These are the questions lenders will ask to learn all about you. By being prepared you will make the lender's job easier. Be prepared to answer the following:

- Why do you need the money?

- What's your current address and telephone number (and landlord's name, address and telephone number if you rent)? If you've lived at your current address for less than two years, what was your previous address?

- What's your employer's name, address and telephone number and your current gross pay? (You'll need a pay slip and may also be asked to provide a letter from your employer confirming your current income.)

- What other income — such as rental income, or dividends — do you have? (Take proof of that income with you, e.g., leases, dividend income statements, etc.)

You must also provide a complete list of all your assets and liabilities:

Assets
- Bank account number and balances. Remember to highlight those accounts and investments you have with the financial institution from which you are trying to borrow.

- Investments such as GICs, term deposits, mutual funds, RRSPs, stocks, real estate, and the amount in each.

- An estimated amount for personal assets such as jewelry, furniture, etc. Don't estimate these high since financial institutions know they have little resale value.

- Make, model and year of your car and its worth.

Liabilities
- Outstanding loans/debts, including to whom you owe money and the amount
  - previous loans
  - credit card balances
  - other forms of financing

- Mortgage statement

Visualize your meeting with the lender. Analyse the information you've put together, identify any areas of weakness (e.g., recent changes in employment) and be prepared to defend them. Analyse your areas of strength (e.g., good cash flow and financial management) and be prepared to emphasize them.

Preparing Your Own Questions

Don't forget, you're the customer. Often, the tables seem to be turned on us when we try to borrow money. We don't feel like the customer anymore. We may feel interrogated and analysed, but often, we don't feel like the customer.

Keep control over the situation. You are offering to buy something, in this case credit. You have a right to be treated like a customer. You should feel positive about the encounter and you should have your questions answered.

Begin by preparing a list of questions you want answered during the interview:

- Are there options to pay off the loan early?
- What terms are available and what's the best term to take?
- What's the best interest rate I can get?
- How often can I make my payments?
- How can I save on interest costs?

Don't start off the interview by firing your list of questions at the lender. Let the lender gather the information he or she needs. By their nature, lenders are conservative and like to feel they are in control. Let the lender take the lead. But get your questions answered. You may be able to ask some of them during the course of the lender's presenting options to you. Check them off as you do. If you appear to be thoroughly prepared, the lender will be impressed by your businesslike manner.

Building Bridges

The loan interview may be your first meeting with the lender. What you say and do during the interview will create an impression on the lender that ultimately will have an impact on the final decision.

A lot has been written about dressing for success. When you go for a loan interview, you're there to sell yourself. How you look will have an impact. You don't have to rush out and spend scads of money on a new suit. But take care when putting yourself together. Part of what you want to communicate is that you're taking the interview seriously and that you want to create a good impression.

Begin by extending your hand for a firm handshake and introducing yourself. Use the lender's name. Smile.

I remember the first time I applied for a loan for a new car. I couldn't believe how nervous I was. My mouth was dry. My hands were clammy. But I knew I had to appear calm. I rolled up a bunch of tissue in my pockets and just before I had to shake hands, I shoved my hands in my pockets and squeezed the tissue to dry off my palms. I shook that man's hand as if I'd taken out dozens of loans and this one was no big deal. Since then, I've borrowed money for lots of other things. I still keep a supply of tissues in my pockets.

You want to create an atmosphere that promotes open conversation. Everyone likes to hear their names used — even lenders. The individual sitting on the other side of the desk is a human being — a person with good days and bad days just like you. Often we think of these people as machines, cogs in the wheel of finance, particularly when we don't get the loan. But the fact is, the lender is a person with a job to do. Lenders have two priorities:

1. They want to help you by providing the financing you need.

2. They want to make sure their decisions are profitable.

Lenders have to carefully balance these priorities to make sure they don't put too much emphasis on either one. They want to

make sure they are making the best possible decision. Remember, it is their other customers' (their depositors') money they are investing. They have to do so with care to ensure both they and their depositors are protected. It's a tough job and they do the best they can.

During the Interview

Just as lenders have two perspectives in dealing with your request for financing, so, too, should you have two perspectives:

1. You need a loan to achieve your objectives.

2. The lender wants to give you that loan, providing it's a good business decision.

As borrowers, we sometimes approach a loan request situation certain the lender wants to deny our requests. When we are denied, we tell ourselves, "I told you so." That's a self-fulfilling prophecy. If you start off believing the lender wants to grant your request, you'll approach the interview situation from a much more positive perspective. The lender will sense your confidence — lenders have great intuition — and the whole experience will be much more positive for you both.

Throughout the interview, be honest and forthright. Present your situation in positive terms. Don't be fearful of the lender, or put him or her on a pedestal. Lenders are human beings who put their socks on one foot at a time, just like you. State your facts calmly and with confidence.

Don't babble or skirt around issues. Lenders have uncanny antennae. If they're not sure why you're behaving a certain way — talking too fast, avoiding important issues, going off on tangents — they may look even more closely at your financial circumstances to find a reason for your discomfort. Of course, they know you may be nervous. They understand and make allowances for that. But they also expect you to be honest and up front with them. They need the answers to the questions they are asking. And they weigh every piece of information you give them against the Five C's of credit to analyse how credit worthy you are.

Speak slowly, and carefully communicate what you have to say. When the lender pauses, don't automatically jump in. Lenders often use silence to invite you to offer more information. Once you've told lenders all *you* want to tell them, don't be influenced into saying more by responding to their silence. If they want more information, let them ask for it.

If lenders seem to be asking a lot of irrelevant questions, don't cut them off and push on. Be patient. Answer any reasonable questions you're asked. If you are concerned about a certain question, politely ask the lender to explain why that information is pertinent. If the explanation is satisfactory, provide the information requested. The lender is simply trying to get to know you. After all, would you lend $20,000 to someone you didn't know?

Even if you are an existing customer of the financial institution and the lender has checked your records, he will still want to form his own impression. Let him.

Your body language is also important. It signals to lenders how you feel about them and about asking for a loan. Studies in the area of communication have shown that people put more stock in your body language than in your words. In fact, listeners receive seven percent of the message from your words, 38 percent from your tone and 55 percent from your body language. That means you must not only sound cool, calm and collected, you must look cool, calm and collected. Smile, sit comfortably without slouching, don't fidget and make good eye contact. That eye contact should be steady, not penetrating.

Concluding the Interview

In concluding the interview, you should:

- Check over the application to ensure that all the information needed has been filled in. Incomplete applications make the credit investigation more difficult and may mean the lender has to contact you again.

- Sign the application. This gives the financial institution your commitment that the information provided is correct. It also gives them permission to do the credit checks necessary to approve the loan.

- Review the terms of the loan you have been discussing to be sure you understand them completely. There is no room for misunderstanding when you're borrowing money.

- Make sure the payment schedule fits with your cash flow. The last thing you need is to put yourself in a position of not being able to repay the loan when you promised. For example, if you are paid on the fifteenth and thirtieth of the month, then that's when the loan payment should come out of your account.

- Find out exactly when the lender will be in touch with you to provide an answer. Don't expect a lender to commit to the loan request on the spot. She can't. But she can give you a firm commitment about when you'll be called with an answer. That should be within 24 hours.

- Make sure the lender knows where you can be reached. If you have a preference in terms of where you should be contacted (at home or at work), tell the lender. Some people prefer to keep their personal lives personal and do not wished to be contacted at the office. But you can't assume the lender will instinctively know this.

- Ask the lender when the best time is to call if you have any more questions. It's not unusual to forget stuff during the stress of the interview. Don't be afraid to call to get something clarified.

- Thank the lender for her time. While you are the customer, saying thank you is a normal courtesy. People who don't leave lenders feeling unappreciated.

Suppose They Turn Me Down?

Most lenders don't take any comfort from having to turn down a loan request. They find it a very difficult task. If you handle the rejection effectively, you can actually build a foundation for a better relationship with the lender for future financing needs.

It's not unusual to be turned down the first time you request financing. After all, you may not have a strong credit history – or any credit history at all. You may not have done enough planning. Or you may not qualify for financing at the current time.

If your request for financing is declined, remember that it is the *request* being denied, not you. Don't take it personally. And don't get angry. You may be frustrated by the fact that your request has been denied, but yelling at the lender won't motivate him to do any more work on your behalf. Instead, find out *why* your request was declined. Ask for details so you can be better prepared the next time you request financing. Be professional. Stay cool.

Take another look at your "request for financing" information, improve your approach and go back again. Work with the lender to find a way to get the loan, or at least find out what you have to do to ensure that a future application will be successful.

6 Business Loans

As the 1980s came to a close, "bigger is better" gave way to "small is beautiful." As unwieldy conglomerates everywhere began to demassify, small business once again became the engine of economic growth and job creation. In this period of economic transition, small business financing has begun to receive a lot of attention, both by the media and by financial institutions.

Whether you are starting a medical or dental practice, or opening up a retail store, you're a small business, providing you have revenues and borrow below a certain level. Typically, those figures are set at about $2 million in revenues and about $500,000 in loan facilities.

Radio, television and newspapers have looked at what financial institutions want in the way of security, the attitudes they display in their interactions with customers, and discrimination in lending. Overall, people have been expressing a high level of dissatisfaction and a lack of understanding about how financial institutions make their decisions with respect to providing financing. People think that banks:

- demand too much in the way of collateral
- charge too much
- don't provide sufficient financing to meet the borrower's needs
- are unwilling to learn about the business, or don't spend enough time analysing earnings potential to ensure a positive outcome for the borrower
- are incapable or unwilling to provide the advice borrowers are seeking
- don't provide consistency in terms of a single person with whom borrowers can deal over the long term
- are uncaring, rude, abrupt, unsympathetic, discriminating, unfair, arrogant…when turning down a request for financing.

Nowhere are issues of discrimination and unfairness more loudly shouted than in the arena of the small business loan — particularly for the start-up of a new business. Often women feel discriminated against simply because they are women. Some business people feel discriminated against because their businesses are small. Overall, the feeling seems to be that the only way to get a loan is to be a man who doesn't need one. Financial institutions have reacted to a lot of negative press by saying that they do not discriminate and that most people applying for a new business loan are simply uneducated in the area of borrowing.

I remember when I applied for my first line of credit for my business. I was told it would be no problem, providing my husband guaranteed the line for me. I was furious. My husband? What did he have to do with it? I was the one applying for the loan. It was *my* business — he wasn't involved in any way. How dare they!

Now, looking back, I realize how uninformed I was. I didn't have a business plan or a projected cash flow. Nor did I have any receivables. Nevertheless, I expected them to give me the line because I hadn't yet proved I wasn't worthy of it. They should just trust me. After all, I knew I was good for it — just ask my mom!

The fact is, when you go off to a financial institution (usually a bank) to apply for a small business loan, you have to go prepared. This is particularly true if it's the first time you will be dealing with the bank. And if you're just out of school, you probably haven't even built up a credit history yet. So banks have very little to go on except how you present your case to them. Whether or not you get the loan depends, in large part, on how well focused and well prepared you are when you go in to ask for the money. It's silly to think, as I did, that you should automatically get the loan because you have yet to mess up. After all, if you were lending your money, would that be your criterion? I think not. So where do you start? By understanding whom you're dealing with.

Understanding Whom You're Dealing With

The first thing you should know is that you'll probably be dealing with a different area of the bank. Personal deposits, loans and investments are typically handled in one area of the bank, while transactions involving small businesses are handled in another. This is often referred to as the "independent business" area of the bank. So, if you've built up a rapport with one area of the bank, you probably can have references supplied, but you'll have to start building bridges with new people.

You should also recognize that you and the lender often come to the table with different objectives and perspectives. You want the money, no matter what. The lender wants to make sure the loan is risk-free, no matter what. You believe you will succeed. After all, why would you bother if you thought you would fail? Lenders, on the other hand, need to be convinced you will succeed where others may have failed. They will approach the whole deal from a much more conservative perspective.

Lenders are people doing a job that places them in a Catch-22. They must balance the need to increase the bank's business volume while maintaining the bank's standards for credit quality. They take these responsibilities very seriously — as you would in their place — and if they err, they do so in favour of a conservative position: they don't lend.

Choosing the Right Lender

When you begin to shop for a lender, make sure you do a thorough job. Your objective should be to choose a lender who understands your business, or is willing to learn about it. To appreciate your challenges, you have to educate the lender about the cycles of your business so he understands the financial, economic and other issues that can have an impact.

Turnover within the financial services industry has always been quite high. The last thing you need is to spend time developing a relationship with a lender, only to find that next week he's moved to another branch or to another institution. Choose a lender who will be there when you need him. This is particularly important if you run into problems. You want a lender who is willing to stick with you through good times and bad. When things get rough, that's not the time to start trying to explain your business, and its ups and downs, to a new lender.

Take time to understand the lender's role in providing you with financing. Ask your lender to describe the bank's lending policies. Insist that he use English, not bankese. For example, banks often place great emphasis on getting timely information on the business in order to monitor the loan. Entrepreneurs with a thousand things to do in 24 hours may not place the same priority on a request for information. Unfortunately, dealing from two different perspectives, banks and borrowers come into conflict over an issue that's simply a matter of priority. However, if you clearly understand why this information is important to your lender, you will be more likely to give it the emphasis it requires. Without a clear understanding, you may have unrealistic expectations about the kind of support you will receive from the bank. Remember, the bank will be trying to minimize its exposure to risk when analysing your application. Knowing that, you can go prepared.

You should expect, and insist on receiving, advice from your banker. This is one area where financial institutions sometimes miss the mark. Some have a policy restricting employees from providing advice. Others provide advice, but do not have people who are sufficiently well trained to provide all the information you need. Shop carefully. You want a financial institution willing to play a partnership role in providing the financial expertise you may be lacking. Unless you are an accountant, you may find much of the financial information and reporting requirements for running a business quite mysterious, so you'll need a relationship with someone who can demystify all this. And you must take responsibility for becoming more skilled in financial matters so that you can contribute to your partnership with the banker.

The Facts of Life

Statistics have shown that 90 percent of all new businesses fail, 80 percent of them within the first two years. I was so aware of this when I started up, that at the beginning of our second year of business, I remember saying to my partner, "If we can make it through this year, we'll be okay." I was sure that the two-year bogeyman was just waiting to pounce on us. I held my breath all the way through year two.

One of the reasons small businesses often fail is that, in many cases, they are owned and operated by only one or two people. As a single owner of a new business, you're the president, the general manager, the sales manager, the personnel manager, the production manager, the purchasing manager, the controller, the researcher, the quality controller, the secretary and the receptionist. To do your job, you have to understand marketing, human relations and finance, not to mention, of course, whatever you're in the business of doing. Needless to say, few of us are experts at everything. In some aspects we shine, in others we have to be content with muddling through.

Your small business also faces uncertainties. Since you're not a big company, well capitalized by the sale of shares, you have to be careful and plan for the problems that come creeping out of the woodwork: not enough customers, employees who are unreliable, outstanding receivables, equipment costs, equipment failure, poor economic conditions, high interest rates, fluctuations in currencies...the list goes on and on. Most banks are well aware of the weakness of new business start-ups and, to protect themselves, will check you over very carefully before giving you their money.

What Banks Want

To convince a lender that the loan you need can be repaid as expected, you must be able to demonstrate that you clearly understand your business, its future needs and how cash flow fluctuations will have an impact. If your assessment is incomplete or painted with too rosy a brush, it is inevitable that the banker's assessment will differ significantly from yours.

Don't be reluctant to tell the lender all about your business, including your plans and financial prospects. Some people are reluctant to tell too much. But if you don't provide the lender with a big-picture perspective, you may be unsuccessful in getting financing.

Essentially, banks want to know that you have a well-thought-out financial proposal, with realistic and achievable objectives. This proposal should include the details of what money you require to achieve your goals, how that money will be used and what security you will offer. Lenders also like to see that you have made contingency plans in the event that everything doesn't go absolutely perfectly. Typically, they want all this information delivered in the form of a "business plan."

Developing a Business Plan

To start with, banks want to know all about your business:

- who you are

  - the company/partnership name, address, telephone number, etc.

  - the shareholders'/partners' names and their personal financial information

  - who does what within the company, their experience and levels of commitment (you might consider including an organizational chart)

  - the name of your lawyer, accountant, banker, etc.

- the products you'll be selling or the services you will be providing
  - what you'll be providing to the marketplace
  - who your suppliers will be
  - the cost of your materials

- the market potential for your products/services
  - who your typical customer is
  - the size of your market
  - how you expect your market to grow/shrink
  - who your competition is and how it will react when you enter the marketplace
  - what differentiates your products/services
  - what your channels of distribution are

- if you're just starting out, when you're planning to hang out your shingle
  - what you have to do to get started
  - your start date

- your facilities (existing or required)
  - details of type of building, square footage and leasing costs
  - equipment needs
  - present/potential capacity
  - how overhead costs have been allocated
  - how you will manage inventory control, inventory on hand and reordering
  - how purchasing will be managed and controlled

- your goals and the activities you will be undertaking in:

    - marketing your product(s) or service(s)

    - production of your products or supply of your services

    - personnel required, expertise needed and estimated payroll costs (how many, unionized, part-time, full-time)

    - finance: what type of financial record-keeping system you'll be using, who will be handling the bookkeeping, how much you'll need to borrow, for what term, by when, and any security you'll be offering

    - administrative considerations: start-up supplies required (e.g., furniture, office supplies, etc.) insurance costs and arrangements, licences required, government approvals, set-up of tax accounts (i.e., GST, PST, corporate tax, employee tax deductions, etc.), and all the rest of the nitpicky stuff.

Much of the information you need to develop a business plan can be found within your business itself, or from a trade association, competitors and customers. Begin by detailing all the

information you have. Then analyse what you don't know and look for help. Don't let pride get in the way of asking for help. Remember, you can't be a specialist in all areas. Start with the people you know, because their information is usually the least expensive. And when you get information you don't particularly want to hear, don't get angry and automatically discount the source of the information. Search for more information to support your position. Use all the tools and people available to you: your partners, employees, accountant, lawyer and suppliers. Then look to trade associations and the Canadian Federation of Independent Business. Look for special interest groups or business clubs, and join those you feel may be helpful.

Your business plan will be very useful in helping you look at the facts and approach the business realistically. It will help you to identify and clearly define your opportunities, the products or services you will offer, your markets and your suppliers. In effect, it provides you with a benchmark against which you can measure your results.

The process of writing down a business plan will also help you to be a better manager. By forcing you to be clear and objective, the business plan creates a realistic starting point. And the impression it creates on the lender will also have an impact. So make sure your presentation is clear, concise, complete and correct. Be balanced in your presentation and always state the downside. If you don't, you leave the worst-case scenario to the lender's imagination.

After you've developed a business plan, the next thing the bank will want to see is a forecast.

Developing a Forecast

A well-developed forecast will demonstrate to a banker how well you know your business and marketplace from a financial perspective. The forecast should, naturally, be realistic, and bankers prefer forecasts to be on the conservative side. Your forecast, along with a budget, will help a lender decide how important the loan is to your business, and your ability to meet your financial obligations. It should contain a forecast of your:

- sales
- cost of goods
- gross profit
- costs for sales and administration
- net profits before taxes

Do a month-by-month forecast for one (the first) year, and then a yearly forecast for the next four years so that, in total, you have a five-year forecast.

Many financial institutions require that you also show them a cash flow projection and projected balance sheet, as well as the assumptions you used in preparing these projected financial statements. These assumptions often cover:

- the basis you used to determine sales
- how you will handle collections
- the terms and conditions for your payables
- your operating expenses (rent, salaries, fixed costs)
- provision for income taxes
- projected capital expenditures
- sources of equity
- your loan requirements, including a projection for the interest rate and repayment schedule

Developing a Cash Flow Forecast

"Cash" refers to the amount of money a business has in its till, in petty cash or in the bank. You must have sufficient cash on hand if you expect to be able to pay your bills and other expenses when they come in, and to account for uncertainties such as unplanned expenses. Without sufficient cash, you may have to delay paying your bills (not good for your corporate credit rating) or, worse, you may become insolvent.

Cash Flow Forecast

for the period: _____

	Month 1	Month 2	Month 3
Add Cash Receipts:			
Cash from sales			
Cash from receivables			
Loan proceeds			
Cash from other sources			
Total Receipts			
Less Disbursements:			
Improvements			
Fixtures & Equipment			
Inventory			
Salaries & ETDs			
Rent			
Utilities			
Maintenance & Repairs			
Advertising			
Insurance			
Delivery			
Loan Repayment			
Income Taxes			
Etc.			
Total Disbursements			
Cash Surplus (Shortage)			
Cash on Hand:			
Beginning of Month			
End of Month			

FIGURE 1

A cash flow forecast illustrates how you expect cash to flow through your business during a period of time, usually six to 12 months, in the future. It details the cash you will receive, and the amount you will spend on a monthly basis. FIGURE 1 shows a cash flow forecast for three months.

Maximizing Your Borrowing Potential

Whether you're setting up a new business or requesting financing (or increased financing) for an existing business, you'll increase your borrowing potential if you offer the lender security for the loan. In some instances, you may be asked to sign personally (to use personal assets such as your home or other personal investments outside the business) to guarantee the loan. Remember, if you do so and the business fails, the financial institution has the right to foreclose on your home/investments to recapture lost funds. If you choose this path, you and your spouse will need separate financial/legal counselling to ensure you are both aware of the repercussions.

You will likely also be asked to use your company's existing or projected assets to secure a loan. These include accounts receivable, inventory, fixed assets and leasehold improvements. The lender may also request performance requirements, referred to as "covenants," which must be met on an annual basis. These covenants may put limits on your expenditures on fixed assets, or may provide a guideline for amounts paid to shareholders or debt to equity ratio (i.e., how much debt the business can carry relative to the amount of equity in the company).

Putting Your Package Together

The key to creating an influential financial proposal is to (a) keep it simple, and (b) provide everything the lender will need to make a well-educated decision. Use a straightforward approach to delivering the basic information (why you need the funds and how they'll be used, as well as the basic information about the company/organization), and provide all the supporting information at the end of the package or in a separate package under the title of "Appendices." Your proposal should emphasize your strengths, but shouldn't ignore the downsides; you want to demonstrate that you understand them clearly and are going into business with both eyes open. In identifying the downsides, show how you would cope with them to indicate to the lender that you have thought out your proposal thoroughly.

There is no such thing as a perfect plan. What you want to achieve is a document that explains your position, shows your intents, thoughts and planning, and demonstrates your commitment to succeeding. You are the person who will make your small business a success. You must believe it so completely you will make your lender believe it too. This plan is a résumé of your knowledge and experience, as well as your estimate of the future. Take care in its preparation and it will serve you well.

Strengthening Your Relationship with Your Banker

Don't become complacent about your relationship with your banker. If things derail, be the first one to tell your banker. He will feel more confident if he hears it from you first. Keep him up to date with your financial information by providing him with cash flow forecasts and financial statements. Invite him to your place of

business and show him around. Help him to understand and develop a real feel for your business.

Don't leave your loan balance just sitting. It will look like you are not committed to managing the loan. If you pay it down and then let it go up again as needed, you will demonstrate that you are actively managing your financing. Discuss your future financing needs with your banker so he will know where you are going and how he can help. And use him as a source of other information. Your banker may be able to help you do credit checks on potential customers or identify areas with potential to complement your business. Your banker may even be able to provide introductions to potential suppliers or customers.

Don't Give Up

If at first you don't succeed, find out why. Ask the lender to explain why you did not get the financing you requested and what you could do differently in the future to achieve your objectives. After all, everything in life is a learning process. It would be a shame to do all that work and simply walk away quietly with nothing to show but a bruised ego.

If you aren't satisfied with the explanation, ask for the loan request to be sent up the line to a higher authority. Explain that your objective is to learn about what you have to do to satisfy the bank and achieve your objectives. If you get no joy, shop around. If you have a well-thought-out plan that is complete, correct, concise and clear, you should at least be able to get an explanation of what else you need to do to qualify. As the customer, you have a right to that information. As a representative of a financial institution, the lender should want to help you qualify in the future. Make sure you're both dealing on a realistic level and that you both are working to the same end: to achieve the financing you need while limiting the risk to the bank.

7 To Borrow or Not to Borrow?

If you've read all the previous chapters you know most of what you need to know about credit, how it works and how to get it. But you still have to make the decision about whether or not to borrow.

Eleven Good Reasons to Borrow

1. *You want to buy a home* — a good reason. A home is likely to be the single largest investment you'll make, and most often it's a good decision, providing you can handle the payments comfortably. As you pay off your mortgage, you'll be building equity in the property. It's like a forced savings plan. And all the while, you'll be able to enjoy your home.

2. *You're financing an education* — a good reason. Whether you are financing your children's education or packing yourself off back to school, you're investing in the future. With increased education comes increased earning potential.

3. *You want to make a contribution to a Registered Retirement Savings Plan* — a good reason. To keep this a sound decision, you should plan to pay off your RRSP loan within one year. Longer than that, and borrowing to contribute doesn't pay.

4. *You're faced with an emergency, but don't have the cash* — a pretty good reason. While this flies in the face of the theory "Never borrow in desperation," you have to be flexible. For genuine emergencies, you may have to borrow. If you're a salesman and your car dies, you may have to borrow to buy a new car just to ensure you can keep making a living. But be certain you take only as much as you absolutely need. Resist the urge to make everything an emergency. And be sure you can work the payments into your cash flow.

5. *You're making home improvements* — a good reason, sometimes. It really depends on the types of home improvements you are making and how comfortably you can work the repayment into your cash flow. If you're making home improvements simply for the enjoyment of your family, the repayment shouldn't cause your cash flow any stress. If you're making improvements to increase the value of your home, make sure they are the right kind of improvements. Adding a pool doesn't increase the value of your home, but renovating your kitchen usually does. Check with real estate agents, and do some research at the library before proceeding.

6. *You want to buy an expensive item* — often a good reason. For the most part, borrowing is an accepted way of financing the purchase of such high-ticket items as cars, major appliances and boats. It makes particular sense if you're taking advantage of a sale or if the purchase will help you save money in the long run. Whatever the item, your primary decision factors should be (a) how easily you can work the repayment into your cash flow, and (b) how much debt you're carrying overall. Think about how you would manage those payments if your financial circumstances changed.

7. *You want to make an investment* — a good reason, providing the investment is sound. Remember, if you borrow to finance an investment and the investment goes into the tank, you're still liable for the debt you've incurred. While interest on investment financing is tax deductible, this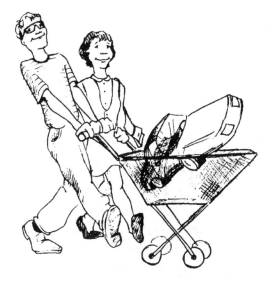

shouldn't be your primary reason for getting into an investment deal. It's still money out of your pocket. Approach this one carefully, get lots of advice and make sure the repayment won't strap you financially.

8. *You want to buy a second property (such as a cottage or investment real estate)* — a good reason. Carefully consider all the tax consequences. The capital gains exemption on property (other than a principal residence) has been eliminated, so property as an investment has become less attractive. Interest on investment property is still tax deductible and property can be a very good investment. A cottage can improve your family's lifestyle and you'll be building up assets, and that's very good.

9. *You want to start a business (or expand an existing business)* — often a very good reason. In the right circumstances, borrowing to start or expand a business is a good idea. You should make sure you are fully aware of both the upsides and downsides of your endeavour. Go into it with both eyes open. If you've done a thorough business plan and cash flow projection — and you've been honest with yourself and your banker — you'll know if this is a good enough reason to borrow.

10. *You're a better borrower than saver* — can be a good reason. Some people find it easier to borrow and pay off their loans, than to save for the things they want. The trick here is to ensure you don't take on more debt than you can handle, and that you leave room in the event of an emergency or investment opportunity.

11. *You're borrowing to consolidate your debts at a lower rate of interest* — good reason. Paying less interest is always a smart move. However, you should be committed to paying off the newly consolidated debt before taking on more (including using your credit cards). If you're not committed to throwing

your cards behind the refrigerator until the loan has been paid off, don't bother consolidating. You'll just be back where you are today (or worse) in a few months.

When to Question Your Motivation to Borrow

Whether or not you qualify for a loan, you should question your borrowing motivation and rationale if:

1. *You aren't sure the usefulness of a purchase will outlast the repayment period.* It's bad enough when we spend cash on impulsive purchases, but when we have to pay for those impulsive actions way beyond the item's life, that can be really hard to take. Ask yourself, and answer honestly, "Will I be severely handicapped without the item?"

2. *An instalment plan makes it too good to pass up.* That's not the right place to start. Begin by deciding whether you need the item at all, and then calculate how much you'll actually be paying in interest.

   Shauna saw an advertisement for a stereo system for $124 a month. She had just moved into a new apartment and desperately wanted a new system. She decided to go for it. When she went to the store, she found out that the system was priced at $1,200. Well, there was no way she could afford that, so she accepted the financing deal. For 24 months, she would pay $124 a month, which she could easily fit into her cash flow.

   At the end of 24 months, Shauna had paid off her stereo. In total she had paid $2,976 ($124 x 24). If she had bought the stereo outright, she would have paid $1,200. In effect, she paid $1,776 in finance charges — more than the actual cost of the stereo system.

   If Shauna had decided to wait a little longer, she could have saved $124 a month in a "stereo account." At the end of nine and a half months she would have had her stereo and saved herself $1,776.

3. *You're adding more debt to your already high debt load.* Piling new debt atop old is dangerous. It can lead you to the point where all your discretionary income is spent making loan payments. Avoid this scenario by setting priorities before borrowing.

4. *You haven't told anyone you intend to borrow.* Making unilateral decisions about financing is a great way to put a strain on your relationships. And if you haven't worked up the guts to tell the most trusted people in your life, maybe it's because you know you won't be able to justify the decision to them. Perhaps you'd like to reconsider?

5. *You're buying something to cheer yourself up.* Lots of people go shopping to lift their spirits. Unfortunately, shopping, like drinking, can create a hangover. Ask yourself whether you'll actually feel better when the bill comes in. Adjust your perspective. Maybe a smaller, less-expensive treat will make you feel just as good.

6. *You're trying to impress others.* Some people need to keep up an image of success. Others shop together to build or strengthen their relationships — a smart little girl I know refers to it humorously as "female bonding." But when it comes to paying off the card or repaying the loan, it isn't so funny. Ask yourself if it's really worth it.

Reviewing Your Situation

Before you decide to borrow, review your financial circumstances to decide whether borrowing is the answer. Perhaps you have enough cash to buy the item outright and save the interest cost. Maybe you have investments that can be liquidated. If you have a term deposit paying you five percent and you're planning to take out a loan at eight percent, your term deposit will actually cost you three percent. You may be better off paying for the item in cash so that there's no financing cost. This is particularly true if the item you plan to buy has a short lifespan.

Check to see if you have assets against which you can borrow. By using your home, life insurance or investments as collateral, the loan will generally cost less.

Analyse how much your investments/savings are earning for you. You'd be surprised at how many people have money in savings accounts paying minimal interest when they could be using equally safe investments such as Canada Savings Bonds, money market mutual funds or cashable term deposits. These all offer fairly high levels of liquidity while generating a higher return.

While reviewing your assets may not provide you with a great source of "hidden" wealth, it can be a very worthwhile exercise. If you have a vacation home, you may decide that by renting that home for a season/year, you may generate enough cash to finance your purchase. Or perhaps you can sell an asset that is not increasing in value or that you fear may decline in value. You'll need to make a list of your assets for your loan interview anyway, so why not start there and determine if there are assets you could use in place of taking a loan?

As part of your financial housekeeping, make a list of all your assets and liabilities and update the list twice a year. Then you can take a quick look to see how you sit financially whenever you're considering borrowing.

Understanding the Cost of Borrowing

Many factors affect the cost of credit to you as a borrower. Lenders obtain their money from depositors (people with savings accounts, term deposits, etc.) or from other financial institutions. That money has to earn a return that is more than they are paying (to their depositors or to the financial institution from whom they borrowed). The difference between what the lender pays for the money and what you are charged for the loan is referred to as the "spread." This spread is expected to cover the operating expenses of the lender and provide a reasonable profit.

The risk of nonpayment is another factor included in the cost of the loan. Typically, financial institutions want to limit their loan losses to .5 percent. That means they have to be right about their decisions to lend 99.5 percent of the time. Financial institutions must ensure their loans are repaid because of their responsibility to their depositors and their shareholders. Consequently, interest rates vary with the level of risk involved for the lender.

You should be very clear on the cost of borrowing. Would you buy a new piece of furniture before looking at the price tag? How about a new car? Before you borrow, make sure you understand how much it will cost. This is where most people slip up when they use their credit cards for financing instead of simply for purchasing convenience. Work out what the financing will cost you over the time the item will be financed. Then decide if you're willing to pay the true price for the item.

Lower Payments over the Long Term versus Higher Payments over the Short

A lower payment made over a longer term may make the loan easier on your cash flow, but it will significantly increase the cost of your purchase. To find out exactly how much you're paying in interest, add up all the monthly payments involved and subtract the purchase price of the item. The difference is the cost of borrowing instead of using cash. If the cost seems high, you might want to reconsider borrowing, or choose a shorter term to reduce the amount of interest you'll be paying.

The More You Borrow, the Lower the Interest Rate

Whether you borrow $1,000 or $100,000, the lender still has the same costs in administering the loan. Therefore, the more you borrow, the lower the administrative cost *per dollar borrowed*, so the lower the interest rate you'll be charged. Not only that, but the likelihood is that the more you qualify to borrow, the lower the risk you are for the lender. The lower the risk of the loan, the less interest you'll pay. That's why big borrowers are often perceived to be more credit worthy than small borrowers.

You can use this to your advantage too. By only borrowing when you need larger sums of money, you can better manage your cash flow and debt. If you set yourself a limit of, say, $10,000 and do not borrow if you need less than that, then you immediately eliminate all the small-ticket purchases you may have previously considered. And the better your credit history, the more likely you will be to qualify for a loan and for a lower interest rate when you do need financing.

Keeping Your Costs Down

1. *Borrow as little as possible during periods of high interest rates.* This may sound pretty obvious, but lots of people just bite the bullet during periods of high interest rates. The higher the rate, the more consideration you should give to whether you should borrow at all.

2. *When rates fall, renegotiate your loan and/or consolidate.* Again, obvious, right? Nope. Lots of people get in the habit of making their loan payments and never think about renegotiating their loans when interest rates have fallen. This doesn't mean running to the bank whenever rates plummet a whole quarter percent. But it does mean keeping an eye on interest rates and taking advantage of changes. And if you're carrying credit card balances, get a consolidation loan to pay them off when rates are lower. And remember to toss your cards behind the refrigerator.

3. *If you have assets you can use as collateral to secure a loan, do it.* The more secure (less risky) the loan is to the lender, the lower the rate of interest you'll pay. Assets used as collateral are still your assets. There may be restrictions on what you can do with them, but they can continue to generate a return for you. The only time they're at risk is if you default on your loan payments, but that's in your control.

4. *Shop hard for rates.* Rates vary (though not substantially) from one financial institution to another. And under the right circumstances, you can usually get a rate that's lower than the posted rate. Shop hard. Negotiate. Offer to consolidate all your business for a better rate.

5. *Avoid a prepayment penalty.* If you can, make sure that when you borrow you have the right to pay off the financing without penalty. Mortgages are a different animal altogether, but you shouldn't have to pay a penalty for prepaying any type of loan.

Can You Afford to Borrow?

Now that you know you need to borrow and how much it'll likely cost you, can you afford it? Your lender will be asking this question, too, when she calculates your debt service ratio. You might as well be prepared for the answer before presenting your situation. (See chapter 4.)

Deciding Which Type of Credit to Use

As mentioned in the introduction, credit in and of itself is neither good nor bad. It's how we use it that counts. If, for example, you use a credit card for short-term (less than 30 days) financing and pay off your balance religiously, you're using that form of credit effectively. But if you don't pay off your credit card balance on time, you are using one of the most expensive forms of credit available.

If you choose to take out a loan for $3,000 to buy furniture, you may not be using that form of credit effectively, either, since the lower the amount you borrow the higher your interest charge will likely be. You would be better off with a personal line of credit, particularly if it's secured.

Make sure you discuss the types of credit available, and which one would be best in your circumstances, with your lender. He or she can provide you with valuable advice about how to minimize the cost of your loan.

Arranging for Credit

Shop around. Find out how interest is calculated and what the cost to you will be in dollars. Make a list of the information you gather so you can compare the options.

Make sure you read the loan agreement so you understand it completely. Ask questions if there are areas about which you are unclear. All blanks on a credit application form should be completed before you sign the document. And if you want to delay signing until you have a chance to discuss the arrangement with an adviser (your parents, a financially astute friend, or your lawyer or accountant), you have the right to do so. Just remember that the lender still needs a certain amount of time to complete the credit investigation before you can be approved for the loan.

Make sure you've got the right type of credit to meet your financing needs. Having done your research and spoken to friends and a couple of lenders, you should be developing a good idea of what you need.

Remember, while you are assessing the lender, he or she is also assessing you. Be realistic about the amount of money you're requesting. Tell the lender everything she needs to know to make an informed decision. Be prepared to provide the documentation the lender needs to support the decision.

Don't Paint Yourself into a Corner

If you find yourself getting deeper and deeper into financial trouble, you should:

- Stop borrowing; that includes using your credit cards, store financing and signing IOUs to your kids. Adding any additional weight to your debt may sink you. Stop and take stock.

- Get in touch with your creditors immediately; let them know you're having difficulty and tell them what steps you're taking to rectify the situation. Creditors don't want to drive you to the brink of bankruptcy, but they can only help you if they know you are willing to discuss your circumstances. Call them before they call you. Be up front. Keep your end of any deal you make.

- Get, and take, advice; you can speak to the lender, to another financial representative or to a credit counsellor. Work out a budget and stick to it.

- Re-evaluate your lifestyle. What got you into the mess? Did you overspend? Did a financial emergency tip the scales? Did you have a budget? Did you stick to it? What are you going to do differently to avoid the problem arising again?

What Happens If You Don't Deal with the Problem

Debt collection practices vary from one creditor to another. Legal steps that can be taken are regulated by provincial law. As a general rule, repossession (seizure) of goods, garnishment and other court actions are covered under provincial law while bankruptcy is covered by federal legislation.

If you default and have offered collateral, creditors have the right to seize the goods and sell them to try to recoup their losses. Even if you haven't offered collateral, creditors may be allowed to seize other goods in order to recover the debt. You usually have plenty of notice and are given one last chance to clear up the debt.

A creditor may also apply for a court order to garnish your wages or bank accounts. If a garnishment is issued, the creditor claims the money you owe directly from your employer or from the financial institution where your accounts are held. You may also be required to pay any court costs.

If the amount owed is quite small, the creditor may choose to sue you in small claims court to recover the debt. Larger amounts usually mean the lender may have to go to a higher court.

If you simply cannot carry on, you may have to declare bankruptcy, or you may be forced to do so by your creditors. Bankruptcy is a legal procedure that releases you from your debts, with a few exceptions (e.g., Revenue Canada).

Bankruptcy allows you to start fresh, but the costs are high. First, many of your personal possessions will be sold to provide creditors with some form of payment. Your credit history will report the bankruptcy for up to seven years, so you'll likely be treated like a leper if you try to apply for credit again too soon. And the bankruptcy will not only affect you financially and emotionally, it will also affect your immediate family, because the family's assets (cars, houses, furniture and the like) will be sold off to satisfy your debts. Of course, if you have no family, no assets and a huge debt, bankruptcy can actually look like a holiday. Just remember, a negative credit reporting history can have a long-lasting effect on your financial picture.

A Final Word on Using Credit Wisely

Sometimes it's easy to forget that you have to pay for what you buy, particularly when you use credit cards for the majority of your purchases. If you want to stay in control of your finances and use credit wisely, here are some guidelines:

- Make a budget and stick to it. Make sure you know how much is coming in and how much is going out each month. Remember to include items that are paid less frequently (such as car and house insurance) or irregularly (such as dental bills).

- Avoid impulse shopping. If you had to use cash to buy the item, would you still buy it? Will you still want it tomorrow? Next week? Next month? Next year?

- Comparison shop for both the items you're buying and the financing you're using. Never buy anything without comparing costs and value.

- Always read and understand any financing arrangements you are signing, particularly store financing arrangements. Understand how much the financing will cost, any fees attached and any penalties you'll have to pay. Know how much interest you'll be paying in dollars.

- Be wary about co-signing or guaranteeing a loan for someone else. If that person defaults, you will be called upon to pay off the loan. Lenders are supposed to advise you of the risks involved in a separate meeting, but ultimately you are responsible for where you put your John Hancock.

- Learn all about credit, how to use it, what it costs and how to choose the right type for your needs. Watch how often you use credit. Be wary of having too many credit cards.

- Keep track of all your credit purchases. Save your receipts or keep a written record of credit card purchases so you can compare them with your statement. Never just pay the statement off without checking it carefully. Mistakes can be made and you may be double-charged, or charged for items you did not purchase.

Now It's Up to You

There you have it — some of the rules and strategies for making credit work for you. Now it's up to you to make sure you're well prepared, practised and professional in how you request financing. Remember to look at your request from the lender's perspective. When you make it easy for the lender to make a positive decision, you both win.

Above all, remember that *you* are the customer. You have the right to shop around. You have the right to be treated as an individual and have your personal needs satisfied. You have the right to explanations all the way along the process. If your rights aren't being acknowledged, shop around. There are lots of lenders out there willing to give you what you need to get what they need.

Don't take no guff! You're the customer!

Glossary

Amortization Period The number of years it takes to repay the entire amount of the financing based on a set of fixed payments.

Appraisal The process of determining the value of a piece of property. Most financial institutions require that property being purchased is appraised before approving a mortgage. For lending purposes, the lower of the sale price or the appraised value is used in determining the allowable mortgage amount.

Assets What you own or can call upon. Often used in determining net worth or in securing financing.

Assumption Agreement A legal document signed by a buyer that requires the buyer assume responsibility for the obligations of an existing mortgage.

Blended Payments Equal payments consisting of both an interest and a principal component. Typically, while the payment amount does not change, the principal portion increases with each payment, while the interest portion decreases.

Canada Mortgage and Housing Corporation (CMHC) The federal Crown corporation that administers the National Housing Act. CMHC services include providing assistance to people and insuring home purchase loans for lenders.

Charge Card A card used for charging purchases. Outstanding balances are due and payable in full immediately upon billing.

Closed Mortgage A mortgage that cannot be prepaid or renegotiated.

Closing Date The date on which the new owner takes possession of the property and the sale becomes final. This is also the date on which the mortgage funds have to be advanced to the customer's solicitor.

Conventional Mortgage A loan that does not exceed 75 percent of the appraised value or purchase price of the property, whichever is less.

Collateral An asset, such as a term deposit, Canada Savings Bond or automobile, that you offer as security for a loan.

Credit Card A form of revolving credit where a minimum payment is required and interest is charged on any outstanding balance.

Credit Scoring A system that assesses a borrower on a number of items, assigning points that are used to determine the borrower's credit worthiness.

Default Failure to repay a mortgage (or loan) based on the specific terms of the mortgage or failure to comply with the terms of the mortgage agreement. When this happens, the lender has the option of foreclosing (see Foreclosure).

Demand Loan A loan where the balance must be repaid upon request.

Deposit A sum of money deposited in trust by the purchaser on making an offer to purchase. When the offer is accepted by the vendor (seller), the deposit is held in trust by a broker, lawyer or notary until the closing of the sale, at which point it is given to the vendor. If a house does not close because of the purchaser's failure to comply with the terms set out in the offer, the purchaser forgos the deposit, and it is given to the vendor as compensation for the breaking of the contract (the offer).

Discharge Indicates the full repayment of the debt against the property. This occurs when customers completely pay off their mortgages, such as at the end of their amortization. (When they sell their homes and do not wish to port their mortgages, it is called a release.)

Equity The excess value of the property over outstanding debts. It is usually the difference between the market value of the property and the outstanding mortgage balance(s).

First Mortgage A debt registered against a property secured by a first charge, or call, on the property.

Fixed-Rate Mortgage A mortgage for which the interest rate is set for the term of the mortgage.

Foreclosure A legal procedure in which the lender takes ownership of the property due to the default of payment by the borrower.

Gross Debt Service (GDS) Ratio Used to determine a borrower's capacity to repay a mortgage, GDS is calculated using the principal, interest, property taxes and heating costs for the property.

Guarantor A person with an established credit rating who guarantees to repay the loan for the borrower if the borrower does not.

High-Ratio Mortgage A loan that exceeds 75 percent of the appraised value or purchase price of the property, whichever is less.

128

Home Equity Line of Credit A personal line of credit secured with the borrower's home equity.

Instalment Loan A loan for a fixed-dollar amount and term with a regular payment schedule.

Interest Adjustment Date (IAD) The date on which the mortgage term will begin. This is usually the first day of the month following the closing date.

Interest-Only Loan A loan on which only the monthly interest cost is paid each month. The full principal balance remains outstanding.

Lost Interest Compensation (LIC) See Prepayment Penalty.

Mortgage A loan that uses a property, such as a house or condominium, as security to ensure the debt is repaid.

Mortgagee The person/financial institution who lends money using a mortgage.

Mortgagor The person who borrows money using a mortgage.

Non-Sufficient Funds (NSF) A cheque drawn against an account in which there is insufficient money to cover the cheque.

Offer to Purchase A legal agreement that details the terms under which the buyer agrees to purchase the property. When accepted by the seller, the offer becomes a legal contract. Some offers are "firm," which means no conditions are attached. Others are "conditional," which means certain conditions, such as financing or inspection, must be met before the offer becomes a binding contract.

Open Mortgage A mortgage that can be repaid at any time without penalty.

Overdraft Protection Revolving credit used primarily to ensure chequing account overdrafts are "covered," eliminating the cost and embarrassment of NSF cheques.

Personal Line of Credit (PLC) A floating- (or variable-) rate loan, which establishes a specific amount of credit available that can be accessed at any time for any purpose.

PI Principal and interest due on a mortgage.

PIN Personal identification number.

PIT Principal, interest and taxes due on a mortgage.

Port To transfer an existing mortgage to a new property.

Prime The lowest rate a financial institution charges its best customers – usually its corporate customers.

Prepayment Penalty A fee charged a borrower by the lender when the borrower prepays all or part of a mortgage more quickly than agreed to under the terms of the mortgage. When current interest rates are lower than when the mortgage was taken, the penalty usually includes an interest penalty (sometimes referred to as a Lost Interest Compensation, Interest Rate Differential or Present Value Loss of Interest).

Principal The original amount of a loan, before interest.

Renegotiating The borrower's changing the mortgage agreement with the existing lender, sometimes done to extend the amortization, reduce or increase the monthly mortgage payments or change the term of the mortgage.

Renewal The borrower's renewal of a mortgage agreement with the same lender. A different term and amortization period may be chosen.

Revolving Credit Open-ended credit (usually to a pre-established credit limit) with no fixed repayment period or amount. Revolving credit may be used whenever the borrower wishes and for any purpose.

Second Mortgage A debt registered against a property that is secured by a second charge on the property. The interest rate charged on a second mortgage is usually higher than that charged on a first mortgage.

Security See Collateral.

Switch To transfer an existing mortgage from one financial institution to another.

Tax Holdback The amount of funds held back from the mortgage advance to cover the property tax billing in full.

Total Debt Service (TDS) Ratio A calculation used to determine a borrower's capacity to repay a loan. TDS is the percentage of the borrower's gross income used to make total monthly payments. See also Gross Debt Service Ratio.

Term The period of time the financing agreement covers.

Variable-Rate Mortgage A mortgage for which the interest rate is fluctuates based on changes in prime.

Vendor Take Back A mortgage provided by the vendor to the buyer.

Index